SPEECHES AGAINST CATILINE I–II

WEARING THE TOGA.
Roman statue at Dresden, of Republican times.
See the note on Chap. XIII, l. 4.

CICERO
IN CATILINAM I & II

Edited with Introduction, Notes and
Vocabulary by
H. E. Gould &
J. L. Whiteley

Published by Bristol Classical Press
General Editor: John H. Betts
(by arrangement with Macmillan Education Ltd.)

Cover illustration: Cicero, from a bust in the
Uffizi Gallery, Florence. [Drawing by Jean Bees.]

Reprinted by permission of Macmillan Education Ltd.

First published by Macmillan & Co. Ltd., 1943

Reprinted by Bristol Classical Press, 1982, 1990
226 North Street
Bedminster
Bristol BS3 1JD

ISBN 0-86292-014-0

Printed in Great Britain by
Short Run Press Ltd., Devon, Exeter

CONTENTS

LIST OF ILLUSTRATIONS

FOREWORD

In preparing this book the editors have followed the scheme which they outlined in the foreword to the first volume in this series, *Civil War in Spain*, viz. a reliable text (in this case the text in the Macmillan Elementary Classics Series and Classical Texts has been very carefully revised), suitable illustrations, a vocabulary that gives only those meanings that are required, and last and perhaps most important of all, adequate assistance in the Notes, so that the student may feel capable of translating with confidence and accuracy.

H. E. G.
J. L. W.

Croydon, 1942.

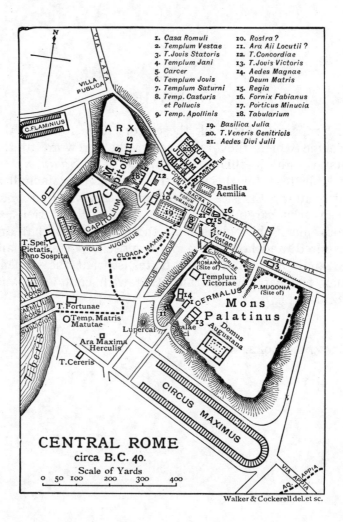

1. Casa Romuli
2. Templum Vestae
3. T. Jovis Statoris
4. Templum Jani
5. Carcer
6. Templum Jovis
7. Templum Saturni
8. Temp. Castoris et Pollucis
9. Temp. Apollinis
10. Rostra?
11. Ara Aii Locutii?
12. T. Concordiae
13. T. Jovis Victoris
14. Aedes Magnae Deum Matris
15. Regia
16. Fornix Fabianus
17. Porticus Minucia
18. Tabularium
19. Basilica Julia
20. T. Veneris Genitricis
21. Aedes Divi Julii

CENTRAL ROME

circa B.C. 40.

Scale of Yards

0   50   100   200   300   400

Walker & Cockerell del. et sc.

INTRODUCTION

(i) Marcus Tullius Cicero

Cicero was born near Arpinum on January 3rd, 106 B.C., and lost his life in December, 43 B.C., in the proscriptions which Antony organised in the troubled period following Caesar's murder. Cicero's life, then, covers the period which saw the collapse of the Roman Republic and the beginning of what was to be the Roman Principate in which the Emperors had the powers of dictators.

He began his career as a lawyer and had such brilliant success at the Roman bar that he was able, although not a member of the governing class, to obtain the regular sequence of magistracies and a seat in the senate. He spent his quaestorship in Sicily, where his conduct was marked by honesty and integrity, and, finally in 51 B.C., he held a provincial governorship in Cilicia, south-east Asia Minor. Cicero's vanity and pride in the fact that he had climbed to the highest offices in the state by his own merit and ability made him deeply attached to the constitutional forms of the Roman Republic, and blinded him to the many political and social evils of the day, such as the narrow-mindedness and selfishness of the ruling class (the senatorial order), its failure to provide a strong and efficient government either in Rome or in the provinces and, above all, its inability to control the successful generals and their armies who were destined to overthrow the Republic.

A short sketch of some of the most important issues at stake in the political sphere during this century will help to make Cicero's position clear.

Theoretically the Roman Republic was democratic in its working, but in reality all the power lay in the hands of a few families identified with the senate, whose ambition it was to retain the reins of government to the exclusion of all others. A generation before Cicero's birth, their political supremacy had been temporarily shaken by two ardent reformers, the brothers, Tiberius and Gaius Gracchus, who seem to have made an honest attempt to solve several serious problems, such as unemployment, the disappearance of the small farmer, and the relations between Rome and her allies in Italy. The senate put every obstacle in their path, and when eventually the Gracchi lost their lives in street fighting, the senatorial order quickly re-established its supremacy. In the first century B.C., however, the senate had to meet further attacks from other reformers, and, as both sides were now resorting to force, they both looked for support to the outstanding general of the day who could get bills passed with the aid of his troops. Thus civil war broke out, which was characterised by cruelty and massacre on both sides.

For example, during the second decade of the first century, when Cicero was just beginning his career at the bar, there were three civil wars, and Rome was twice besieged and captured by Roman generals in command of Roman and Italian troops. More terrible still, in 80 B.C., Sulla began the system of ' proscriptions ', under which all those whose political opinions were regarded as dangerous to the winning side could be killed with impunity.

The next twenty years, 80–60 B.C., were momentous in the history of the Roman Republic. Sulla's attempt to bolster up the power of the senate gradually collapsed before attacks from several quarters, especially from Pompey and Caesar, the latter of whom was beginning to take an active part in politics.

During this period, too, Cicero had established his reputation as a lawyer and orator, and, in particular, he had distinguished himself by a successful prosecution of Verres for misgovernment in Sicily. At this time, also, he entered political life, became aedile in 69, praetor in 66, and consul in 63 B.C. His consular year of office will always be remembered for the vigorous way in which he crushed a dangerous attempt to effect a *coup d'état* on the part of Catiline, an unscrupulous noble who hoped to rally to his side the many discontented elements in Italy. The fact that there was so much discontent in Italy is a strong indictment of the senatorial government of the preceding seventy years.

Cicero attempted to form a strong government, capable of maintaining order in Rome and the provinces, and of controlling the recklessness of demagogic tribunes and their irresponsible followers among the landless and workless in Rome. He aimed at establishing a kind of ' National Government ', a combination of senators, business men and financiers, and

PLATE OF COINS

SILVER COIN (57 B.C.)

Showing the head of Sulla, and inscribed SULLA CO(n)S(ul).

SILVER COIN (44 B.C.)

Showing portrait of Julius Caesar wearing a laurel wreath. The inscription runs CAESAR DICT(ator) PERPETVO.

GOLD COIN (42–38 B.C.)

Showing portrait of Pompey and Pompey and his eldest son Gnaius. The inscriptions are MAG(nus) PIVS IMP(erator) ITER(um) and continued on the reverse PRAEF(ectus) CLAS(sis) ET OR(ae) MARIT(imae).

BRONZE COIN (after 30 B.C.)

Showing a head of Cicero's only son. There is some resemblance between it and the busts of his father, shown in the frontispiece.

SILVER COIN (28 B.C.)

Celebrating the capture of Egypt by Octavian (29 B.C.). The inscription on the obverse is CAESAR COS VI. The crocodile is the symbol of Egypt.

the upper classes in the Italian cities, protected by a loyal general and a strong force of troops. He cast Pompey for the role of protector of the constitution.

Such a plan, however, failed to work. In the first place, in 60 B.C., the alliance between Caesar, Pompey and Crassus, known as the First Triumvirate, showed that the senate had now lost all power of independent action. Secondly, there was Julius Caesar to be reckoned with, an ambitious man who gradually came to realise that the Roman Republic was too far gone for remedial treatment, and should be replaced by a new system.

Thus, during the next sixteen years, 60–44 B.C., Cicero's political ideal was completely shattered. He himself was exiled in 58 [1] and recalled in 57 B.C. During 58–51 B.C. Caesar was adding to the Roman province a new and rich Empire, Gaul, which he annexed after a brilliant series of campaigns. In Rome itself, constitutional government broke down and anarchy became so widespread that the senate had to call in Pompey and his troops to restore order. Gradually the senate succeeded in alienating Pompey from Caesar, and in 49 B.C. civil war broke out between Caesar and the senate, led by Pompey.

It took Caesar four years to crush the senatorial party, and by 45 B.C. he was virtually the sole ruler of the Roman Empire. A year later, he was assassinated by a group of senators led by Brutus, who seems to have honestly believed that, with Caesar removed, the Roman Republic would be restored to its former position.

[1] The reason for his exile was that during his consulship in 63 B.C., he had executed without trial certain fellow-conspirators of Catiline.

If we are to understand Cicero's feelings at this time, his distress at his exile, his unrestrained joy at his recall, his dismay at the dictatorial position of Julius Caesar, and his delight at his murder, we have to remember that to Cicero a political career in what he considered a free state with democratic forms of government was the only legitimate career for a free man. He could never forget that he himself had risen to the top and obtained the consulship and a seat in the senate by his own ability and merit. He failed to see, as Caesar saw clearly enough, that the Republic was past mending. Thus after Caesar's murder, Cicero attempted once more to form a 'National Government'. Not only did he fail again, but he lost his own life. For he had embittered Antony, Caesar's successor, and, when the Second Triumvirate was formed, consisting of Antony, Lepidus and Octavian, Antony got his revenge by having Cicero's name put down on the list of the proscribed.

(ii) L. Sergius Catiline and the Catilinarian Conspiracies

L. Sergius Catiline was born of a patrician family in 108 B.C., and was thus two years older than Cicero. Both our contemporary authorities (Cicero and Sallust, who wrote a monograph on him) testify to his tremendous mental and physical powers and to the depraved immorality of his youth. But we must discount many of the horrible crimes which Cicero imputed to Catiline in his own partisan electoral speech, and which, if true, would make him one of the worst monsters of mankind.

Again, both our authorities mention Catiline's rare gift of making loyal friends and the versatility of his character, which enabled him to mix easily with all types of men and win the support even of good men, as Cicero says,[1] by the appearance, so to speak, of an assumed virtue. Unfortunately for Rome, Catiline lacked the rich inheritance which would easily have enabled a man of his birth, drive, and ambition to attain to the highest offices of state.

But his attitude to such political honours was fundamentally different from Cicero's. Catiline regarded them as a birth-right, which, if he could not obtain them by fair means, he meant to have by violence. Moreover, the opportunities for enrichment, especially as a governor of some rich province after his consular office, were necessary for an aristocrat of his type to restore his bankrupt and mortgaged fortunes.

He first appeared in public life as a devoted partisan of Sulla in the Sullan proscriptions of 80 B.C., and in 68 B.C. he secured the praetorship. The following year he spent as governor in N. Africa, but he acted in such an oppressive manner that, even before his year of office terminated, native envoys had made strong representations to the senate about his scandalous behaviour. These accusations were a severe blow to his hopes of obtaining the consulship of 65 B.C., because they prevented his being accepted as a candidate. Hence arose what came to be known as the First Catilinarian Conspiracy. Allying himself with two other rejected nominees who had been found guilty of bribery, Catiline formed the hare-brained scheme of

[1] See the fine picture in Cic., *pro Caelio*, 13.

murdering the incoming consuls and other prominent senators on the 1st January 65 B.C., and then of seizing the consular power for himself and his associates. As, however, the conspirators failed to maintain any secrecy, the execution of their plans was postponed until the following month, and even then miscarried because, it is said, Catiline gave the signal too soon to the conspirators, who had not yet appeared with sufficiently large numbers of armed men.

In 65 B.C. Catiline had to stand his trial for mis-government in N. Africa, and, although he obtained a favourable verdict by buying off his accuser and bribing the jury, he was again debarred from standing for the consulship, i.e. of 64 B.C. By this time he was deeply in debt, and he seems to have been taken up by Crassus, a very wealthy and ambitious financier, who was on the look-out for men like Catiline whom he could use for his own ends. He had already won his support by enabling him and his fellow-conspirators to escape punishment for the First Catilinarian Conspiracy.

Financed by Crassus, who had marked him out as a pos-sible military leader against his rival Pompey,[1] Catiline appeared as a candidate for the consulship of 63 B.C. In addition to four other candidates, there was the successful lawyer and orator Cicero, whose otherwise strong prospects were weakened by the fact that he was a *novus homo*, ' a new man ', i.e. one who did not belong to the governing classes. The latter distrusted Cicero for his previous support of Pompey, and, in any

---

[1] Pompey, who was conducting a successful campaign against Mithridates, a powerful prince in Asia Minor, was likely to return to Italy that year.

case, were not willing to admit even talented men
within their own circle. Yet Cicero was one of the
elected consuls and Catiline again failed,—a failure
which was as much due to his own unscrupulous
behaviour before the elections as to the fact that the
senate may have been alarmed over his real designs
and the part which Crassus was playing behind the
scenes.

Catiline was now completely exasperated and in
danger of financial ruin. In 63 B.C. he was again a candidate for the consulship, i.e. of 62 B.C., and, no longer
enjoying the financial support of Crassus, he openly
based his candidature on a programme of *novae tabulae*,
' a clean slate ', or cancellation of debts, and made a
strong appeal to Sullan veterans who had sunk into
debt, and, above all, to the many aristocrats who had
been made bankrupt by their heavy expenditure in
seeking office,[1] an expenditure which was inevitable if
they wished to keep these political honours among
themselves. Thus, viewed as a piece of legislation, this
scheme of Catiline can only be dubbed as reactionary.

Catiline's chances of success were weakened by a
financial panic, by his own arrogant and overweening
behaviour, and by the firm attitude of the consul Cicero.
In his first Catilinarian Oration, the latter tells us how
he persuaded the senate to put off the elections for a
few days, and how he appeared at the elections armed
with his own cuirass and protected by a bodyguard of
young equites, and thus prevented the electors from
being panicked. Catiline failed again.

[1] E.g., electoral expenses such as bribes to electors, and the
pay-roll of a vast army of clients.

B

His reply was that of the man whose patience is exhausted, an attempted *coup de main*, known as the Second Catilinarian Conspiracy, in which it is interesting to note first, that of sixteen known conspirators twelve were of senatorial standing, and second that the main object for many was not so much the seizure of political power as the remission of debts.

Catiline's plans were as follows : to maintain in Rome a hired band of gladiators and to arouse the Sullan veterans and other discontented elements in Etruria under the leadership of an experienced Sullan centurion, named Manlius. The force of Manlius was to advance on Praeneste and then on the 27th October to effect a night march on Rome. On the following day, there was to be a joint rising in Rome by the troops of Manlius and Catiline's gladiators.

Unfortunately for the success of this *coup d'état*, Cicero learned of these plans through a secret agent, a woman, named Fulvia. Thereupon he summoned the senate and was authorised by it to make full enquiries.

On October 21st, after reports had been received that Manlius was mustering his army, Cicero again summoned the senate, which after two days' discussion, proclaimed a state of emergency and gave the consuls unrestricted powers to provide for the safety of the state by their resolution, *videant consules ne quid res publica detrimenti capiat*, ' let the consuls see to it that the state suffer no harm '.

Thus empowered, Cicero acted vigorously. He moved the gladiators to Capua, called out the municipal levies, and commissioned the praetor Metellus Celer to raise fresh levies in Northern Italy. But, lacking complete evidence, he felt himself unable to arrest Catiline. In any case, as a *novus homo*, one who was still not sure of the support of the governing class to which he did not belong, Cicero did not dare to risk making a mistake, for, as has been well said, the aristocrats no doubt objected to their being saved by an ' outsider '.

His previous plans thus checked, Catiline at first protested his innocence and offered to place himself under voluntary arrest. Then he resolved on even more desperate action. Slipping out from custody and, no doubt, with the connivance of his gaoler, M. Metellus, on the night of November 6th-7th, he met several of the conspirators at the house of one, Laeca, ' in the Sickle-makers' Street '. There he matured his new plans, announced his intended departure from Rome to join Manlius, decided who was to stay behind in Rome, allotted the various roles each conspirator had to play in the riots, murders, and conflagrations that were to follow, and finally gave to two Roman knights the task of assassinating Cicero. The latter, however, was warned in time by the same secret agent, prevented his own murder, and on November 8th, delivered the First Catilinarian Oration before the senate in the presence of Catiline himself. In it, he denounced him as an arch-fiend and the bane of his country, disclosed all his new plans, and implored him to rid his country of his presence. It is probable that, in making this request, the consul was hoping to force the senate's hand and make it say, ' No! arrest him at once.' But the senators did not give him that support.

The next day, Catiline left Rome, ostensibly, under protest, for Marseilles and voluntary exile, but in reality to join Manlius. Then followed the Second Catilinarian Oration in which Cicero hailed his departure as a glorious victory, expressed his hope that, with the ringleader departed, the conspiracy would collapse, and endeavoured to persuade the conspirators still left behind to give up their mad schemes and ambitions.

But his hopes were not fulfilled. Catiline continued to carry on a vigorous recruiting campaign in Etruria, while the conspirators in Rome, led by P. Cornelius Lentulus, made plans to murder Cicero and the leading senators, to set the city on fire, to call out the slaves and lower orders to loot, and then to break through to Catiline.

Cicero again got news of these moves, this time through some envoys from the Allobroges, a Gallic tribe in South-East France, whom the conspirators had approached with a view to their joining in the revolt. By their agency, the consul succeeded in getting written evidence of the conspiracy, and obtained from the senate the power to have the leading conspirators in Rome arrested. After a long debate in which Julius Caesar intervened and suggested perpetual custody for the conspirators in Italian towns, the senate at last decided on capital punishment.

Cicero's Third Catilinarian Oration, which he delivered to the people, gives the details of the events leading up to the arrest of the conspirators, while his Fourth Oration, delivered in the senate during the debate mentioned in the last paragraph, merely examines the question whether the conspirators should be executed or not, from the point of view of his own personal safety.

At the beginning of the next year, 62 B.C., Catiline was killed, fighting bravely at the head of his forces.

This short account of the Catilinarian Conspiracies may be concluded with one additional note. Attempts have been made to represent Catiline as a true reformer, i.e. as one who was the legitimate successor of the Gracchi brothers, of Saturninus, Drusus, and Sulpicius, men who had tried to solve some of the pressing problems to which reference has been made in the introduction, p. x. Modern views, however, tend to reject these attempts as a complete misconception of the facts and maintain the traditional idea that Catiline was a man of great power both mental and physical, but obstinate, amoral, and reactionary.

(iii) THE WORKS OF CICERO

The works of Cicero may be divided into three groups : (i) his speeches, both legal and political, by which he established an undisputed reputation as the master of Roman eloquence ; (ii) his voluminous correspondence, which gives us a picture of Roman political and social life under the later republic, more vivid and varied than that of any other period of Roman history ; and finally (iii) his philosophical works, in which he aimed at explaining and criticising for the benefit of educated Romans the doctrines and tenets of the leading Greek philosophical schools. Under (iii) we may classify the two essays on ' Old Age ' and ' Friendship '.

This volume in the 'Modern School Classics' contains the first two of the four speeches Cicero delivered against Catiline, the first on November 8th, 63 B.C., in the Temple of Jupiter Stator, before the senate, and the second before the people on the following day, when Catiline had voluntarily left Rome, ostensibly to go into exile, but in reality to join Manlius.

All the speeches were published later by Cicero himself, and, though no doubt he carefully revised and edited them, they may be taken to represent most of what Cicero himself said. They have always been popular, as the number of extant manuscripts copied during the Middle Ages shows, and, as they are not too difficult, they make an excellent introduction to Cicero's oratorical works. In them can be found most of the characteristics of his style, his perfect mastery of the Latin tongue, his brilliant powers of description and narration, and his irony and sarcasm.

M. TULLI CICERONIS

INVECTIVARUM IN L. CATILINAM

LIBRI DUO

ORATIO PRIMA

HABITA IN SENATU

Cicero attacks Catiline for his insolent audacity, and deplores the spirit of the time which allows this enemy of the state to continue his activities unmolested.

I. 1. Quo usque tandem abutere, Catilina, patientia nostra? quam diu etiam furor iste tuus nos eludet? quem ad finem sese effrenata iactabit audacia? Nihilne te nocturnum praesidium Palatii, nihil urbis vigiliae, nihil timor populi, nihil concursus bonorum omnium, 5 nihil hic munitissimus habendi senatus locus, nihil horum ora vultusque moverunt? Patere tua consilia non sentis? constrictam iam horum omnium scientia teneri coniurationem tuam non vides? Quid proxima, quid superiore nocte egeris, ubi fueris, quos con- 10 vocaveris, quid consilii ceperis, quem nostrum ignorare arbitraris? 2. O tempora, o mores! senatus haec intellegit, consul videt: hic tamen vivit. Vivit? immo vero etiam in senatum venit, fit publici consilii particeps, notat et designat oculis ad caedem unum 15 quemque nostrum. Nos autem, fortes viri, satis facere rei publicae videmur, si istius furorem ac tela vitemus. Ad mortem te, Catilina, duci iussu consulis iam pridem oportebat, in te conferri pestem quam tu in nos

1

20 machinaris. 3. An vero vir amplissimus, P. Scipio,
pontifex maximus, Ti. Gracchum, mediocriter labefactantem statum rei publicae, privatus interfecit :
Catilinam, orbem terrae caede atque incendiis vastare
cupientem, nos consules perferemus? Nam illa nimis
25 antiqua praetereo, quod C. Servilius Ahala Sp. Maelium, novis rebus studentem, manu sua occidit. Fuit,
fuit ista quondam in hac re publica virtus, ut viri
fortes acrioribus suppliciis civem perniciosum quam
acerbissimum hostem coërcerent. Habemus senatus
30 consultum in te, Catilina, vehemens et grave ; non
deest rei publicae consilium neque auctoritas huius
ordinis : nos, nos, dico aperte, consules desumus.

*In spite of many precedents which justify his execution, Catiline
still lives, because Cicero is unwilling to act against him until he
has the full support of the country.*

II. 4. Decrevit quondam senatus, ut L. Opimius
consul videret ne quid res publica detrimenti caperet :
nox nulla intercessit ; interfectus est propter quasdam
seditionum suspiciones C. Gracchus, clarissimo patre,
5 avo, maioribus ; occisus est cum liberis M. Fulvius
consularis. Simili senatus consulto C. Mario et L.
Valerio consulibus est permissa res publica ; num
unum diem postea L. Saturninum tribunum pl. et
C. Servilium praetorem mors ac rei publicae poena
10 remorata est? At vero nos vicesimum iam diem
patimur hebescere aciem horum auctoritatis. Habemus enim huiusce modi senatus consultum, verum
inclusum in tabulis, tamquam in vagina reconditum,
quo ex senatus consulto confestim te interfectum esse,

15 Catilina, convenit. Vivis, et vivis non ad deponen-
dam, sed ad confirmandam audaciam. Cupio, patres
conscripti, me esse clementem, cupio in tantis rei
publicae periculis me non dissolutum videri, sed iam
me ipse inertiae nequitiaeque condemno. 5. Castra
20 sunt in Italia contra populum Romanum in Etruriae
faucibus collocata, crescit in dies singulos hostium
numerus, eorum autem castrorum imperatorem ducemque hostium intra moenia atque adeo in senatu videtis
intestinam aliquam cotidie perniciem rei publicae moli-
25 entem. Si te iam, Catilina, comprehendi, si interfici
iussero, credo, erit verendum mihi, ne non potius hoc
omnes boni serius a me quam quisquam crudelius factum
esse dicat. Verum ego hoc, quod iam pridem factum
esse oportuit, certa de causa nondum adducor ut
30 faciam. Tum denique interficiere, cum iam nemo
tam improbus, tam perditus, tam tui similis inveniri
poterit, qui id non iure factum esse fateatur. 6. Quam
diu quisquam erit qui te defendere audeat, vives, sed
vives ita, ut vivis, multis meis et firmis praesidiis
35 obsessus, ne commovere te contra rem publicam possis.
Multorum te etiam oculi et aures non sentientem, sicut
adhuc fecerunt, speculabuntur atque custodient.

*Catiline, however, is beset on all sides, so that all his schemes
and plans are known and his actions anticipated.*

III. Etcnim quid est, Catilina, quod iam amplius
exspectes, si neque **nox** tenebris obscurare coetus
nefarios nec privata domus parietibus continere voces
coniurationis tuae potest? si illustrantur, si erumpunt
5 omnia? Muta iam istam mentem, mihi crede : obli-

viscere caedis atque incendiorum. Teneris undique ;
luce sunt clariora nobis tua consilia omnia, quae iam
mecum licet recognoscas. 7. Meministine me ante
diem XII Kalendas Novembres dicere in senatu, fore
10 in armis certo die, qui dies futurus esset ante diem
VI Kalendas Novembres, C. Manlium, audaciae satellitem atque administrum tuae? Num me fefellit,
Catilina, non modo res tanta, tam atrox tamque
incredibilis, verum, id quod multo magis est admiran-
15 dum, dies? Dixi ego idem in senatu, caedem te
optimatium contulisse in ante diem V Kalendas
Novembres, tum cum multi principes civitatis Roma
non tam sui conservandi quam tuorum consiliorum
reprimendorum causa profugerunt. Num infitiari
20 potes te illo ipso die meis praesidiis, mea diligentia
circumclusum commovere te contra rem publicam
non potuisse, cum tu discessu ceterorum nostra tamen,
qui remansissemus, caede te contentum esse dicebas?
8. Quid? cum te Praeneste Kalendis ipsis Novembribus
25 occupaturum nocturno impetu esse confideres, sen-
sistine illam coloniam meo iussu meis praesidiis,
custodiis, vigiliis esse munitam? Nihil agis, nihil
moliris, nihil cogitas, quod non ego non modo audiam,
sed etiam videam planeque sentiam.

*The events of the ' night before last ' at the house of Marcus
Laeca—when the details of the conspiracy are outlined and
the murder of Cicero the next morning is plotted.*

IV. Recognosce tandem mecum noctem illam
superiorem : iam intelleges multo me vigilare acrius
ad salutem quam te ad perniciem rei publicae. Dico
te priore nocte venisse inter falcarios—non agam

obscure—in M. Laecae domum ; convenisse eodem 5
complures eiusdem amentiae scelerisque socios. Num
negare audes ? quid taces? convincam, si negas ;
video enim esse hic in senatu quosdam qui tecum
una fuerunt. 9. O di immortales! ubinam gentium
sumus? in qua urbe vivimus? quam rem publicam 10
habemus? Hic, hic sunt in nostro numero, patres
conscripti, in hoc orbis terrae sanctissimo gravissimo-
que consilio, qui de nostro omnium interitu, qui de
huius urbis atque adeo de orbis terrarum exitio cogitent. Hos ego video consul et de re publica sententiam 15
rogo, et quos ferro trucidari oportebat, eos nondum
voce vulnero. Fuisti igitur apud Laecam illa nocte,
Catilina ; distribuisti partes Italiae ; statuisti quo
quemque proficisci placeret, delegisti quos Romae
relinqueres, quos tecum educeres, discripsisti urbis 20
partes ad incendia, confirmasti te ipsum iam esse
exiturum, dixisti paulum tibi esse etiam nunc morae,
quod ego viverem. Reperti sunt duo equites Romani
qui te ista cura liberarent et sese illa ipsa nocte paulo
ante lucem me in meo lectulo interfecturos esse 25
pollicerentur. 10. Haec ego omnia, vixdum etiam
coetu vestro dimisso, comperi ; domum meam maioribus praesidiis munivi atque firmavi ; exclusi eos,
quos tu ad me salutatum mane miseras, cum illi ipsi
venissent, quos ego iam multis ac summis viris ad me 30
id temporis venturos esse praedixeram.

Catiline is urged to leave Rome at once and cleanse the city
of himself and his villainous associates.

V. Quae cum ita sint, Catilina, perge quo coepisti,
egredere aliquando ex urbe ; patent portae : proficiscere. Nimium diu te imperatorem tua illa Manliana castra desiderant. Educ tecum etiam omnes
5 tuos, si minus, quam plurimos ; purga urbem. Magno
me metu liberabis, dum modo inter me atque te murus

GOLD COIN OF THE EMPEROR ANTONINUS PIUS (A.D. 138–161).
inscribed to Iovi Statori, ' to Jupiter Stator '. The god is
holding a sceptre in his left hand and a thunderbolt
in his right.

intersit. Nobiscum versari iam diutius non potes :
non feram, non patiar, non sinam. 11. Magna dis
immortalibus habenda est atque huic ipsi Iovi Statori,
10 antiquissimo custodi huius urbis, gratia, quod hanc
tam taetram, tam horribilem tamque infestam rei
publicae pestem totiens iam effugimus. Non est
saepius in uno homine summa salus periclitanda rei
publicae. Quam diu mihi, consuli designato, Catilina,
15 insidiatus es, non publico me praesidio, sed privata
diligentia defendi. Cum proximis comitiis consularibus me consulem in campo et competitores tuos
interficere voluisti, compressi conatus tuos nefarios

amicorum praesidio et copiis, nullo tumultu publice
concitato ; denique, quotienscumque me petisti, per 20
me tibi obstiti, quamquam videbam perniciem meam
cum magna calamitate rei publicae esse coniunctam.
12. Nunc iam aperte rem publicam universam petis ;
templa deorum immortalium, tecta urbis, vitam
omnium civium, Italiam totam ad exitium et vasti- 25
tatem vocas. Quare quoniam id, quod est primum
et quod huius imperii disciplinaeque maiorum proprium est, facere nondum audeo, faciam id, quod est
ad severitatem lenius et ad communem salutem
utilius. Nam si te interfici iussero, residebit in re 30
publica reliqua coniuratorum manus ; sin tu, quod te
iam dudum hortor, exieris, exhaurietur ex urbe tuorum
comitum magna et perniciosa sentina rei publicae.
13. Quid est, Catilina? num dubitas id me imperante
facere, quod iam tua sponte faciebas? Exire ex urbe 35
iubet consul hostem. Interrogas me : num in exsilium? Non iubeo, sed, si me consulis, suadeo.

*Nothing in Rome can bring Catiline happiness or pleasure, for
the scandals of his private and public life are known to
all, and his attempts on the life of Cicero and other leading
men have been foiled.*

VI. Quid est enim, Catilina, quod te iam in hac
urbe delectare possit? in qua nemo est extra istam
coniurationem perditorum hominum qui te non
metuat, nemo qui non oderit. Quae nota domesticae
turpitudinis non inusta vitae tuae est? quod priva- 5
tarum rerum dedecus non haeret in fama? quae
libido ab oculis, quod facinus a manibus umquam
tuis, quod flagitium a toto corpore afuit? cui tu

adulescentulo, quem corruptelarum illecebris irretisses,
10 non aut ad audaciam ferrum aut ad libidinem facem
praetulisti? 14. Quid vero? nuper, cum morte superioris uxoris novis nuptiis domum vacuefecisses, nonne
etiam alio incredibili scelere hoc scelus cumulasti?
quod ego praetermitto et facile patior sileri, ne in hac
15 civitate tanti facinoris immanitas aut exstitisse aut
non vindicata esse videatur. Praetermitto ruinas
fortunarum tuarum, quas omnes proximis Idibus tibi
impendere senties : ad illa venio, quae non ad privatam ignominiam vitiorum tuorum, non ad domesticam
20 tuam difficultatem ac turpitudinem, sed ad summam
rem publicam atque ad omnium nostrum vitam
salutemque pertinent. 15. Potestne tibi haec lux,
Catilina, aut huius caeli spiritus esse iucundus, cum
scias esse horum neminem qui nesciat, te pridie
25 Kalendas Ianuarias Lepido et Tullo consulibus stetisse
in comitio cum telo? manum consulum et principum
civitatis interficiendorum causa paravisse? sceleri ac
furori tuo non mentem aliquam aut timorem tuum,
sed fortunam populi Romani obstitisse? Ac iam illa
30 omitto—neque enim sunt aut obscura aut non multa
commissa postea— : quotiens tu me designatum,
quotiens vero consulem interficere conatus es! quot
ego tuas petitiones ita coniectas, ut vitari posse non
viderentur, parva quadam declinatione et, ut aiunt,
35 corpore effugi! Nihil agis, nihil adsequeris, neque
tamen conari ac velle desistis. 16. Quotiens tibi iam
extorta est ista sica de manibus! quotiens excidit
casu aliquo et elapsa est! quae quidem quibus abs
te initiata sacris ac devota sit, nescio, quod eam
40 necesse putas esse in consulis corpore defigere.

Catiline is feared and hated by his fellow-citizens and by his
native land. Therefore the only thing for him to do is to rid
his country of his presence by going into exile.

VII. Nunc vero quae tua est ista vita? Sic enim
iam tecum loquar, non ut odio permotus esse videar,
quo debeo, sed ut misericordia, quae tibi nulla debetur.
Venisti paulo ante in senatum. Quis te ex hac tanta
frequentia, tot ex tuis amicis ac necessariis salutavit? 5
Si hoc post hominum memoriam contigit nemini, vocis
exspectas contumeliam, cum sis gravissimo iudicio
taciturnitatis oppressus? Quid, quod adventu tuo ista
subsellia vacuefacta sunt, quod omnes consulares, qui
tibi persaepe ad caedem constituti fuerunt, simul 10
atque adsedisti, partem istam subselliorum nudam
atque inanem reliquerunt, quo tandem animo hoc
tibi ferendum putas? 17. Servi mehercule mei si
me isto pacto metuerent, ut te metuunt omnes cives
tui, domum meam relinquendam putarem: tu tibi 15
urbem non arbitraris? et si me meis civibus iniuria
suspectum tam graviter atque offensum viderem,
carere me adspectu civium quam infestis omnium
oculis conspici mallem: tu cum conscientia scelerum
tuorum agnoscas odium omnium iustum et iam diu 20
tibi debitum, dubitas, quorum mentes sensusque
vulneras, eorum adspectum praesentiamque vitare?
Si te parentes timerent atque odissent tui neque eos
ulla ratione placare posses, ut opinor, ab eorum oculis
aliquo concederes: nunc te patria, quae communis 25
est parens omnium nostrum, odit ac metuit et iam
diu nihil te iudicat nisi de parricidio suo cogitare:
huius tu neque auctoritatem verebere nec iudicium
sequere nec vim pertimesces? 18. Quae tecum, Catilina,

30 sic agit et quodam modo tacita loquitur : ' Nullum
iam aliquot annis facinus exstitit nisi per te, nullum
flagitium sine te ; tibi uni multorum civium neces,
tibi vexatio direptioque sociorum impunita fuit ac
libera ; tu non solum ad neglegendas leges et quaes-
35 tiones, verum etiam ad evertendas perfringendasque
valuisti. Superiora illa, quamquam ferenda non
fuerunt, tamen, ut potui, tuli : nunc vero me totam
esse in metu propter unum te, quidquid increpuerit
Catilinam timeri, nullum videri contra me consilium
40 iniri posse, quod a tuo scelere abhorreat, non est
ferendum. Quam ob rem discede atque hunc mihi
timorem eripe, si est verus, ne opprimar, sin falsus,
ut tandem aliquando timere desinam.'

*Catiline's offer to place himself under arrest has been rejected
by prominent citizens. Therefore, he should go into exile—
a suggestion that is approved by the silence of the senate, and
the shouts of the crowd outside.*

VIII. 19. Haec si tecum ita, ut dixi, patria loquatur, nonne impetrare debeat, etiam si vim adhibere
non possit? Quid, quod tu te ipse in custodiam
dedisti? quod vitandae suspicionis causa ad M'.
5 Lepidum te habitare velle dixisti? a quo non receptus
etiam ad me venire ausus es atque ut domi meae te
adservarem rogasti. Cum a me quoque id responsum
tulisses, me nullo modo posse isdem parietibus tuto
esse tecum, qui magno in periculo essem, quod isdem
10 moenibus contineremur, ad Q. Metellum praetorem
venisti : a quo repudiatus ad sodalem tuum, virum
optimum, M. Metellum demigrasti, quem tu videlicet
et ad custodiendum diligentissimum et ad suspicandum

sagacissimum et ad vindicandum fortissimum fore
putasti. Sed quam longe videtur a carcere atque a15
vinculis abesse debere, qui se ipse iam dignum custodia
iudicarit?

20. Quae cum ita sint, Catilina, dubitas, si emori
aequo animo non potes, abire in aliquas terras et
vitam istam, multis suppliciis iustis debitisque erep- 20
tam, fugae solitudinique mandare? ' Refer' inquis ' ad
senatum '; id enim postulas et, si hic ordo sibi placere
decreverit te ire in exsilium, obtemperaturum te esse
dicis. Non referam, id quod abhorret a meis moribus,
et tamen faciam ut intellegas, quid hi de te sentiant. 25
Egredere ex urbe, Catilina, libera rem publicam metu,
in exsilium, si hanc vocem exspectas, proficiscere.
Quid est, Catilina? ecquid attendis, ecquid animad-
vertis horum silentium? Patiuntur, tacent. Quid
exspectas auctoritatem loquentium, quorum volun- 30
tatem tacitorum perspicis? 21. At si hoc idem huic
adulescenti optimo, P. Sestio, si fortissimo viro,
M. Marcello, dixissem, iam mihi consuli hoc ipso in
templo senatus iure optimo vim et manus intulisset.
De te autem, Catilina, cum quiescunt, probant, cum 35
patiuntur, decernunt, cum tacent, clamant; neque
hi solum, quorum tibi auctoritas est videlicet cara,
vita vilissima, sed etiam illi equites Romani, honestis-
simi atque optimi viri, ceterique fortissimi cives,
qui circumstant senatum, quorum tu et frequentiam 40
videre et studia perspicere et voces paulo ante ex-
audire potuisti. Quorum ego vix abs te iam diu
manus ac tela contineo, eosdem facile adducam, ut
te haec, quae vastare iam pridem studes, relinquentem
usque ad portas prosequantur. 45

Such appeals are useless : yet he should go into exile, if only to bring unpopularity upon Cicero ; for open war will only increase the consul's reputation.

IX. 22. Quamquam quid loquor? te ut ulla res frangat? tu ut umquam te corrigas? tu ut ullam fugam meditere? tu ut ullum exsilium cogites? Utinam tibi istam mentem di immortales duint! Tametsi
5 video, si mea voce perterritus ire in exsilium animum induxeris, quanta tempestas invidiae nobis, si minus in praesens tempus, recenti memoria scelerum tuorum, at in posteritatem impendeat. Sed est tanti, dum modo ista sit privata calamitas et a rei publicae periculis
10 seiungatur. Sed tu ut vitiis tuis commoveare, ut legum poenas pertimescas, ut temporibus rei publicae cedas, non est postulandum. Neque enim is es, Catilina, ut te aut pudor umquam a turpitudine aut metus a periculo aut ratio a furore revocaverit. 23. Quam
15 ob rem, ut saepe iam dixi, proficiscere ac, si mihi inimico, ut praedicas, tuo conflare vis invidiam, recta perge in exsilium : vix feram sermones hominum, si id feceris, vix molem istius invidiae, si in exsilium iussu consulis ieris, sustinebo. Sin autem servire
20 meae laudi et gloriae mavis, egredere cum importuna sceleratorum manu, confer te ad Manlium, concita perditos cives, secerne te a bonis, infer patriae bellum, exsulta impio latrocinio, ut a me non eiectus ad alienos, sed invitatus ad tuos isse videaris. 24. Quam-
25 quam quid ego te invitem, a quo iam sciam esse praemissos, qui tibi ad Forum Aurelium praestolarentur armati? cui sciam pactam et constitutam cum Manlio diem? a quo etiam aquilam illam argenteam, quam tibi ac tuis omnibus confido perniciosam ac funestam

futuram, cui domi tuae sacrarium scelerum con- 30
stitutum fuit, sciam esse praemissam? Tu ut illa
carere diutius possis, quam venerari ad caedem pro-
ficiscens solebas, a cuius altaribus saepe istam impiam
dexteram ad necem civium transtulisti?

Such a war is one for which Catiline is suited by nature,
upbringing, and training.

X. 25. Ibis tandem aliquando, quo te iam pridem
ista tua cupiditas effrenata ac furiosa rapiebat ;
neque enim tibi haec res adfert dolorem, sed quandam
incredibilem voluptatem. Ad hanc te amentiam
natura peperit, voluntas exercuit, fortuna servavit. 5
Numquam tu non modo otium, sed ne bellum quidem
nisi nefarium concupisti. Nactus es ex perditis atque
ab omni non modo fortuna, verum etiam spe derelictis
conflatam improborum manum. 26. Hic tu qua
laetitia perfruere ! quibus gaudiis exsultabis! quanta 10
in voluptate bacchabere, cum in tanto numero tuorum
neque audies virum bonum quemquam neque videbis.
Ad huius vitae studium meditati illi sunt qui feruntur
labores tui, iacere humi non solum ad obsidendum
stuprum, verum etiam ad facinus obeundum, vigilare 15
non solum insidiantem somno maritorum, verum
etiam bonis otiosorum. Habes, ubi ostentes tuam
illam praeclaram patientiam famis, frigoris, inopiae
rerum omnium, quibus te brevi tempore confectum
esse senties. 27. Tantum profeci tum, cum te a 20
consulatu reppuli, ut exsul potius temptare quam
consul vexare rem publicam posses, atque ut id, quod
esset a te scelerate susceptum, latrocinium potius quam
bellum nominaretur.

The complaints of Rome described : ' Why does Cicero allow such a brigand to be at large? Nothing in the history of the state, not even the fear of unpopularity, should prevent his using the strictest measures against him'.

XI. Nunc ut a me, patres conscripti, quandam prope iustam patriae querimoniam detester ac deprecer, percipite, quaeso, diligenter quae dicam, et ea penitus animis vestris mentibusque mandate. Etenim si 5 mecum patria, quae mihi vita mea multo est carior, si cuncta Italia, si omnis res publica sic loquatur : ' M. Tulli, quid agis? Tune eum, quem esse hostem comperisti, quem ducem belli futurum vides, quem exspectari imperatorem in castris hostium sentis, 10 auctorem sceleris, principem coniurationis, evocatorem servorum et civium perditorum, exire patiere, ut abs te non emissus ex urbe, sed immissus in urbem esse videatur? Nonne hunc in vincla duci, non ad mortem rapi, non summo supplicio mactari imperabis? 15 28. Quid tandem te impedit? Mosne maiorum? At persaepe etiam privati in hac re publica perniciosos cives morte multarunt. An leges, quae de civium Romanorum supplicio rogatae sunt? At numquam in hac urbe, qui a re publica defecerunt, civium iura 20 tenuerunt. An invidiam posteritatis times? Praeclaram vero populo Romano refers gratiam, qui te, hominem per te cognitum, nulla commendatione maiorum tam mature ad summum imperium per omnes honorum gradus extulit, si propter invidiae aut 25 alicuius periculi metum salutem civium tuorum neglegis. 29. Sed si quis est invidiae metus, non est vehementius severitatis ac fortitudinis invidia quam inertiae ac nequitiae pertimescenda. An cum bello

vastabitur Italia, vexabuntur urbes, tecta ardebunt,
30 tum te non existimas invidiae incendio conflagra-
turum? '

*Cicero's reply : it is not the fear of unpopularity, but the lack
of support in the house that makes him cautious.   Thus he
seeks to compel Catiline to declare himself by his own actions
as the enemy of his country.*

XII. His ego sanctissimis rei publicae vocibus et
eorum hominum qui hoc idem sentiunt, mentibus
pauca respondebo. Ego, si hoc optimum factu
iudicarem, patres conscripti, Catilinam morte multari,
5 unius usuram horae gladiatori isti ad vivendum non
dedissem. Etenim si summi viri et clarissimi cives
Saturnini et Gracchorum et Flacci et superiorum com-
plurium sanguine non modo se non contaminarunt, sed
etiam honestarunt, certe verendum mihi non erat,
10 ne quid hoc parricida civium interfecto invidiae in
posteritatem redundaret. Quodsi ea mihi maxime
impenderet, tamen hoc animo fui semper, ut invidiam
virtute partam gloriam, non invidiam putarem.
30. Quamquam non nulli sunt in hoc ordine, qui aut
15 ea quae imminent non videant, aut ea quae vident
dissimulent ; qui spem Catilinae mollibus sententiis
aluerunt coniurationemque nascentem non credendo
corroboraverunt ; quorum auctoritate multi, non
solum improbi, verum etiam imperiti, si in hunc
20 animadvertissem, crudeliter et regie factum esse
dicerent. Nunc intellego, si iste, quo intendit, in
Manliana castra pervenerit, neminem tam stultum
fore qui non videat coniurationem esse factam,
neminem tam improbum qui non fateatur. Hoc

autem uno interfecto intellego hanc rei publicae 25
pestem paulisper reprimi, non in perpetuum comprimi posse.   Quodsi se eiecerit secumque suos eduxerit
et eodem ceteros undique collectos naufragos adgre-
garit, exstinguetur atque delebitur non modo haec
tam adulta rei publicae pestis, verum etiam stirps ac 30
semen malorum omnium.

Catiline's departure with his associates to the camp of Manlius
will enable the government to root out once and for all this
cancer from the vitals of the state.   Cicero closes with a
confident appeal for protection to Jupiter Stator.

XIII.   31. Etenim iam diu, patres conscripti, in his
periculis coniurationis insidiisque versamur, sed nescio
quo pacto omnium scelerum ac veteris furoris et
audaciae maturitas in nostri consulatus tempus erupit.
Quodsi ex tanto latrocinio iste unus tolletur, videbimur 5
fortasse ad breve quoddam tempus cura et metu esse
relevati, periculum autem residebit et erit inclusum
penitus in venis atque in visceribus rei publicae.   Ut
saepe homines aegri morbo gravi, cum aestu febrique
iactantur, si aquam gelidam biberunt, primo relevari 10
videntur, deinde multo gravius vehementiusque ad-
flictantur, sic hic morbus, qui est in re publica, relevatus
istius poena, vehementius reliquis vivis ingravescet.
32. Qua re secedant improbi, secernant se a bonis,
unum in locum congregentur, muro denique, quod 15
saepe iam dixi, secernantur a nobis ; desinant insidiari
domi suae consuli, circumstare tribunal praetoris
urbani, obsidere cum gladiis curiam, malleolos et
faces ad inflammandam urbem comparare : sit denique
inscriptum in fronte unius cuiusque, quid de re publica 20

sentiat. Polliceor hoc vobis, patres conscripti, tantam in nobis consulibus fore diligentiam, tantam in vobis auctoritatem, tantam in equitibus Romanis virtutem, tantam in omnibus bonis consensionem, ut Catilinae 25 profectione omnia patefacta inlustrata, oppressa vindicata esse videatis.

33. Hisce ominibus, Catilina, cum summa rei publicae salute, cum tua peste ac pernicie cumque eorum exitio, qui se tecum omni scelere parricidioque 30 iunxerunt, proficiscere ad impium bellum ac nefarium. Tu, Iuppiter, qui isdem quibus haec urbs auspiciis a Romulo es constitutus, quem Statorem huius urbis atque imperii vere nominamus, hunc et huius socios a tuis ceterisque templis, a tectis urbis ac moenibus, 35 a vita fortunisque civium omnium arcebis, et homines bonorum inimicos, hostes patriae, latrones Italiae, scelerum foedere inter se ac nefaria societate con- iunctos, aeternis suppliciis vivos mortuosque mactabis.

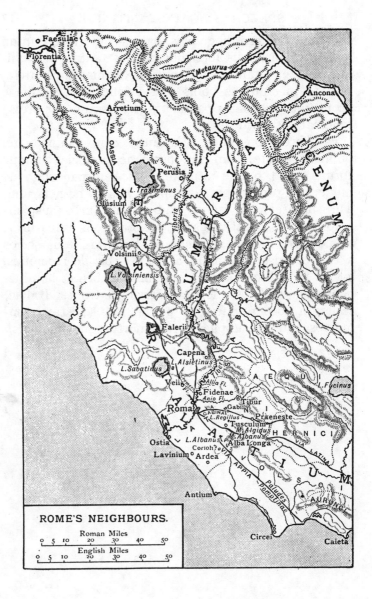

ROME'S NEIGHBOURS.

Roman Miles
0 5 10   20   30   40   50

English Miles
0 5 10   20   30   40   50

ORATIO SECUNDA

HABITA AD POPULUM

Cicero acclaims the departure of Catiline from Rome as an outstanding victory—a victory which is as painful to Catiline as it is joyful to the city.

I. 1. Tandem aliquando, Quirites, L. Catilinam, furentem audacia, scelus anhelantem, pestem patriae nefarie molientem, vobis atque huic urbi ferrum flammamque minitantem, ex urbe vel eiecimus, vel emisimus, vel, ipsum egredientem, verbis prosecuti sumus. 5 Abiit, excessit, evasit, erupit. Nulla iam pernicies a monstro illo atque prodigio moenibus ipsis intra moenia comparabitur. Atque hunc quidem unum, huius belli domestici ducem, sine controversia vicimus. Non enim iam inter latera nostra sica illa 10 versabitur : non in Campo, non in foro, non in curia, non denique intra domesticos parietes, pertimescemus. Loco ille motus est, cum est ex urbe depulsus : palam iam cum hoste, nullo impediente, bellum iustum geremus. Sine dubio perdidimus hominem, magni- 15 ficeque vicimus, cum illum ex occultis insidiis in apertum latrocinium coniecimus. 2. Quod vero non cruentum mucronem, ut voluit, extulit, quod vivis nobis egressus est, quod ei ferrum de manibus extorsimus, quod incolumes cives, quod stantem urbem 20 reliquit ; quanto tandem illum maerore adflictum esse et profligatum putatis? Iacet ille nunc prostratus, Quirites, et se perculsum atque abiectum esse sentit ;

19

et retorquet oculos profecto saepe ad hanc urbem, quam ex suis faucibus ereptam esse luget ; quae 25 quidem laetari mihi videtur, quod tantam pestem evomuerit, forasque proiecerit.

Catiline has long deserved death—a punishment which, though it might have aroused some sympathy for his cause, Cicero would not have hesitated to inflict. But his departure now declares him as an open enemy of the state. It is a pity that he did not take all his supporters with him.

II. 3. At, si quis est talis quales esse omnes oportebat, qui in hoc ipso in quo exsultat et triumphat oratio mea, me vehementer accuset, quod tam capitalem hostem non comprehenderim potius quam emiserim, non est ista mea culpa, Quirites, sed tem- 5 porum. Interfectum esse L. Catilinam et gravissimo supplicio adfectum iam pridem oportebat, idque a me et mos maiorum et huius imperii severitas et res publica postulabat. Sed quam multos fuisse putatis qui quae ego deferrem non crederent? quam multos 10 qui etiam defenderent? Ac si illo sublato depelli a vobis omne periculum iudicarem, iam pridem ego L. Catilinam non modo invidiae meae, verum etiam vitae periculo sustulissem. 4. Sed cum viderem, ne vobis quidem omnibus re etiam tum probata, si illum, 15 ut erat meritus, morte multassem, fore ut eius socios invidia oppressus persequi non possem, rem huc deduxi, ut tum palam pugnare possetis, cum hostem aperte videretis. Quem quidem ego hostem, Quirites, quam vehementer foris esse timendum putem, licet 20 hinc intellegatis, quod etiam illud moleste fero, quod ex urbe parum comitatus exierit. Utinam ille omnes

secum suas copias eduxisset! Tongilium mihi eduxit,
quem amare in praetexta coeperat, Publicium et
25 Minucium, quorum aes alienum contractum in popina
nullum rei publicae motum adferre poterat : reliquit
quos viros! quanto aere alieno, quam valentes, quam
nobiles!

*Catiline's army is weak compared with the forces which are or
can be marshalled against him. But his supporters within
the city are dangerous. Fortunately their designs are known
and will be severely repressed.*

III. 5. Itaque ego illum exercitum prae Gallicanis
legionibus et hoc dilectu, quem in agro Piceno et
Gallico Q. Metellus habuit, et his copiis quae a nobis
cotidie comparantur, magno opere contemno, collec-
5 tum ex senibus desperatis, ex agresti luxuria, ex
rusticis decoctoribus, ex eis qui vadimonia deserere
quam illum exercitum maluerunt : quibus ego non
modo si aciem exercitus nostri, verum etiam si edictum
praetoris ostendero, concident. Hos, quos video voli-
10 tare in foro, quos stare ad curiam, quos etiam in
senatum venire, qui nitent unguentis, qui fulgent
purpura, mallem secum eduxisset : qui si hic
permanent, mementote non tam exercitum illum
esse nobis quam hos qui exercitum deseruerunt,
15 pertimescendos. Atque hoc etiam sunt timendi magis,
quod quid cogitent me scire sentiunt, neque tamen
permoventur. 6. Video, cui sit Apulia attributa, quis
habeat Etruriam, quis agrum Picenum, quis Gallicum,
quis sibi has urbanas insidias caedis atque incendiorum
20 depoposcerit ; omnia superioris noctis consilia ad me
perlata esse sentiunt ; patefeci in senatu hesterno

die ; Catilina ipse pertimuit, profugit : hi quid exspectant? Ne illi vehementer errant, si illam meam pristinam lenitatem perpetuam sperant futuram.

Cicero will make them one concession : they may leave Rome and join Catiline. Thus the city will be purged of all those undesirables with whom he has been so intimate and over whom he has such powerful influence.

IV. Quod exspectavi, iam sum adsecutus, ut vos omnes factam esse aperte coniurationem contra rem publicam videretis : nisi vero si quis est qui Catilinae similes cum Catilina sentire non putet. Non est 5 iam lenitati locus ; severitatem res ipsa flagitat. Unum etiam nunc concedam : exeant ; proficiscantur ; ne patiantur desiderio sui Catilinam miserum tabescere. Demonstrabo iter : Aurelia via profectus est : si accelerare volent, ad vesperam consequentur. 7. O 10 fortunatam rem publicam, si quidem hanc sentinam huius urbis eiecerit! Uno mehercule Catilina exhausto, relevata mihi et recreata res publica videtur. Quid enim mali aut sceleris fingi aut excogitari potest, quod non ille conceperit? quis tota Italia veneficus, 15 quis gladiator, quis latro, quis sicarius, quis parricida, quis testamentorum subiector, quis circumscriptor, quis ganeo, quis nepos, quis adulter, quae mulier infamis, quis corruptor iuventutis, quis corruptus, quis perditus inveniri potest qui se cum Catilina non 20 familiarissime vixisse fateatur? Quae caedes per hosce annos sine illo facta est? quod nefarium stuprum non per illum? 8. Iam vero quae tanta in ullo unquàm homine iuventutis illecebra fuit, quanta in illo? qui alios ipse amabat turpissime, aliorum amori

flagitiosissime serviebat, aliis fructum libidinum, aliis 25
mortem parentum, non modo impellendo, verum
etiam adiuvando, pollicebatur. Nunc vero quam
subito, non solum ex urbe, verum etiam ex agris,
ingentem numerum perditorum hominum collegerat!
Nemo, non modo Romae, sed nec ullo in angulo totius 30
Italiae, oppressus aere alieno fuit, quem non ad hoc
incredibile sceleris foedus adsciverit.

Similarly, he was always a favourite with scoundrels of the worst
   type, a reckless, bankrupt, and dissolute band. The severe
   punishment they will receive will bring peace and security to
   the country.

V. 9. Atque, ut eius diversa studia in dissimili
ratione perspicere possitis, nemo est in ludo gladiatorio
paulo ad facinus audacior qui se non intimum Catilinae esse fateatur ; nemo in scaena levior et nequior
qui se non eiusdem prope sodalem fuisse com- 5
memoret. Atque idem tamen, stuprorum et
scelerum exercitatione adsuefactus frigore et fame
et siti ac vigiliis perferendis, fortis ab istis prae-
dicabatur, cum industriae subsidia atque instrumenta
virtutis in libidine audaciaque consumeret. 10

10. Hunc vero si secuti erunt sui comites, si ex
urbe exierint desperatorum hominum flagitiosi greges,
o nos beatos, o rem publicam fortunatam, o praeclaram
laudem consulatus mei! Non enim iam sunt mediocres hominum libidines, non humanae et tolerandae 15
audaciae : nihil cogitant nisi caedes, nisi incendia, nisi
rapinas. Patrimonia sua profuderunt, fortunas suas
obligaverunt, res eos iampridem, fides deficere nuper
coepit : eadem tamen illa, quae erat in abundantia,

20 libido permanet. Quod si in vino et alea comissationes
solum et scorta quaererent, essent illi quidem des-
perandi, sed tamen essent ferendi. Hoc vero quis
ferre possit, inertes homines fortissimis viris insidiari,
stultissimos prudentissimis, ebrios sobriis, dormientes
25 vigilantibus? Qui mihi accubantes in conviviis,
complexi mulieres impudicas, vino languidi, conferti
cibo, sertis redimiti, unguentis obliti, debilitati stupris,
eructant sermonibus suis caedem bonorum atque
urbis incendia.

30 11. Quibus ego confido impendere fatum aliquod, et
poenam, iamdiu improbitati, nequitiae, sceleri, libidini
debitam aut instare iam plane aut certe iam adpro-
pinquare. Quos si meus consulatus, quoniam sanare
non potest, sustulerit, non breve nescio quod tempus,
35 sed multa saecula propagarit rei publicae. Nulla est
enim natio quam pertimescamus, nullus rex qui
bellum populo Romano facere possit ; omnia sunt
externa unius virtute terra marique pacata : domesticum bellum manet, intus insidiae sunt, intus in-
40 clusum periculum est, intus est hostis : cum luxuria
nobis, cum amentia, cum scelere certandum est. Huic
ego me bello ducem profiteor, Quirites ; suscipio
inimicitias hominum perditorum : quae sanari poterunt, quacumque ratione sanabo ; quae resecanda
45 erunt, non patiar ad perniciem civitatis manere.
Proinde aut exeant aut quiescant aut, si et in urbe et
in eadem mente permanent, ea quae merentur ex-
spectent.

On a Roman lamp.

From a Pompeian Wall Painting.

GLADIATORS

**Note the details of the armour, the dropped shield, which denotes
defeat, and the appeal to the spectators for mercy.**

*Some may say that Cicero has driven Catiline into exile, as
though he were the man to be frightened of the consul's speech.
He realised the feeling in the senate yesterday, when Cicero
revealed all his plans. Of course Manlius' camp does not
expect him! He has gone to Massilia into voluntary exile.*

VI. 12. At etiam sunt qui dicant, Quirites, a me
eiectum in exsilium esse Catilinam. Quod ego si
verbo adsequi possem, istos ipsos eicerem, qui haec
loquuntur. Homo enim videlicet timidus aut etiam
5 permodestus vocem consulis ferre non potuit : simul
atque ire in exsilium iussus est, paruit, ivit. Hesterno
die, Quirites, cum domi meae paene interfectus essem,
senatum in aedem Iovis Statoris convocavi, rem
omnem ad patres conscriptos detuli : quo cum Catilina
10 venisset, quis eum senator appellavit? quis salutavit?
quis denique ita aspexit ut perditum civem, ac non
potius ut importunissimum hostem? quin etiam
principes eius ordinis partem illam subselliorum, ad
quam ille accesserat, nudam atque inanem reliquerunt.
15 Hic ego vehemens ille consul, qui verbo cives in
exsilium eicio, quaesivi a Catilina, in nocturno con-
ventu apud M. Laecam fuisset necne. 13. Cum
ille, homo audacissimus, conscientia convictus primo
reticuisset, patefeci cetera : quid ea nocte egisset,
20 quid in proximam constituisset, quem ad modum
esset ei ratio totius belli descripta, edocui. Cum
haesitaret, cum teneretur, quaesivi, quid dubitaret
proficisci eo, quo iam pridem pararet, cum arma,
cum secures, cum fasces, cum tubas, cum signa mili-
25 taria, cum aquilam illam argenteam, cui ille etiam
sacrarium domi suae fecerat, scirem esse praemissam.
14. In exsilium eiciebam, quem iam ingressum esse

ROMAN SILVER COIN (55 B.C.), showing *sella curulis*, official chair of Roman magistrates, and *fasces* and *secures*.

ROMAN SILVER COIN (58 B.C.), showing consul, walking between two lictors, carrying the *fasces*.

FASCES
(*Relief in the Capitoline Museum*)

The rods bound into a *fascis*, to which was added an axe, were carried as emblems of authority by the *lictors* in attendance on the higher Roman magistrates.

in bellum videbam? Etenim, credo, Manlius iste
centurio, qui in agro Faesulano castra posuit, bellum
30 populo Romano suo nomine indixit, et illa castra nunc
non Catilinam ducem exspectant, et ille eiectus in exsilium se Massiliam, ut aiunt, non in haec castra conferet.

*The task of government is not easy, for if Catiline abandons his
plans, Cicero's counter-measures will be mis-interpreted.
But he will not go into exile, he will declare war, though some
of his supporters may still fear that he is on his way to
Massilia and not to the camp of Manlius.*

VII. O condicionem miseram non modo adminis-
trandae, verum etiam conservandae rei publicae!
Nunc si L. Catilina consiliis, laboribus, periculis meis
circumclusus ac debilitatus subito pertimuerit, sen-
5 tentiam mutaverit, deseruerit suos, consilium belli
faciendi abiecerit, et ex hoc cursu sceleris ac belli iter
ad fugam atque in exsilium converterit, non ille a me
spoliatus armis audaciae, non obstupefactus ac perterritus mea diligentia, non de spe conatuque depulsus,
10 sed indemnatus innocens in exsilium eiectus a consule
vi et minis dicetur, et erunt qui illum, si hoc fecerit,
non improbum, sed miserum, me non diligentissimum
consulem, sed crudelissimum tyrannum existimari
velint. 15. Est mihi tanti, Quirites, huius invidiae
15 falsae atque iniquae tempestatem subire, dum modo a
vobis huius horribilis belli ac nefarii periculum de-
pellatur. Dicatur sane eiectus esse a me, dum modo
eat in exsilium, sed, mihi credite, non est iturus.
Nunquam ego a dis immortalibus optabo, Quirites,
20 invidiae meae levandae causa, ut L. Catilinam ducere
exercitum hostium atque in armis volitare audiatis

sed triduo tamen audietis ; multoque magis illud
timeo ne mihi sit invidiosum aliquando quod illum
emiserim potius quam quod eiecerim. Sed cum sint
homines qui illum cum profectus sit eiectum esse 25
dicant, idem, si interfectus esset, quid dicerent?
16. Quamquam isti, qui Catilinam Massiliam ire dic-
titant, non tam hoc queruntur, quam verentur.
Nemo est istorum tam misericors qui illum non
ad Manlium quam ad Massilienses ire malit. Ille 30
autem si mehercule hoc quod agit nunquam ante
cogitasset, tamen latrocinantem se interfici mallet
quam exsulem vivere. Nunc vero, cum ei nihil adhuc
praeter ipsius voluntatem cogitationemque acciderit,
nisi quod vivis nobiṣ Roma profectus est, optemus 35
potius ut eat in exsilium quam queramur.

*Cicero seeks to win back some of Catiline's supporters who have
     remained in Rome. In all, there are several classes, of
     whom the first has large debts, but larger estates which they
     do not realise will be completely lost, if Catiline is successful.*

VIII. 17. Sed cur tam diu de uno hoste loquimur
et de eo hoste qui iam fatetur se esse hostem, et quem,
quia quod semper volui, murus interest, non timeo ;
de his, qui dissimulant, qui Romae remanent, qui
nobiscum sunt, nihil dicimus? quos quidem ego, si 5
ullo modo fieri possit, non tam ulcisci studeo quam
sanare sibi ipsos, placare rei publicae : neque id quare
fieri non possit, si me audire volent, intellego. Ex-
ponam enim vobis, Quirites, ex quibus generibus
hominum istae copiae comparentur : deinde singulis 10
medicinam consilii atque orationis meae, si quam
potero, adferam.

18. Unum genus est eorum, qui magno in aere
alieno maiores etiam possessiones habent, quarum
15 amore adducti dissolvi nullo modo possunt. Horum
hominum species est honestissima, sunt enim locupletes,
voluntas vero et causa impudentissima. Tu agris, tu
aedificiis, tu argento, tu familia, tu rebus omnibus
ornatus et copiosus sis, et dubites de possessione
20 detrahere, adquirere ad fidem? Quid enim exspectas?
bellum? quid ergo? in vastatione omnium tuas possessiones sacrosanctas futuras putas? An tabulas
novas? errant, qui istas a Catilina exspectant. Meo
beneficio tabulae novae proferuntur, verum auctiona-
25 riae ; neque enim isti qui possessiones habent alia
ratione ulla salvi esse possunt. Quod si maturius
facere voluissent neque, id quod stultissimum est,
certare cum usuris fructibus praediorum, et locuple-
tioribus his et melioribus civibus uteremur. Sed
30 hosce homines minime puto pertimescendos, quod aut
deduci de sententia possunt aut, si permanebunt,
magis mihi videntur vota facturi contra rem publicam
quam arma laturi.

*The second class of his supporters is also deeply in debt, but
being more ambitious, hopes to retrieve its fallen fortunes by
a revolution and a share in the spoils. A forlorn hope in
the face of the consuls, the power of the senate and the
assistance of heaven! Revolution, too, means, if it is
successful, the supremacy of the lowest types.*

*The third class, mostly Sullan veterans, are actuated by
the same motives, but the citizens remember previous outbreaks
and will not tolerate a similar situation.*

IX. 19. Alterum genus est eorum, qui quamquam
premuntur aere alieno, dominationem tamen exspec-

tant, rerum potiri volunt, honores, quos quieta
re publica desperant, perturbata consequi se posse
arbitrantur. Quibus hoc praecipiendum videtur, unum 5
scilicet et idem quod reliquis omnibus, ut desperent
se id quod conantur consequi posse; primum omnium me ipsum vigilare, adesse, providere rei publicae;
deinde, magnos animos esse in bonis viris, magnam
concordiam, maximam adesse multitudinem, magnas 10
praeterea copias militum; deos denique immortales
huic invicto populo, clarissimo imperio, pulcherrimae
urbi contra tantam vim sceleris praesentes auxilium
esse laturos. Quod si iam sint id, quod summo furore
cupiunt, adepti, num illi in cinere urbis et sanguine 15
civium, quae mente conscelerata ac nefaria con-
cupierunt, se consules aut dictatores aut etiam reges
sperant futuros? Non vident id se cupere, quod si
adepti sint, fugitivo alicui aut gladiatori concedi sit
necesse?   20

20. Tertium genus est aetate iam adfectum, sed
tamen exercitatione robustum, quo ex genere est ipse
Manlius, cui nunc Catilina succedit. Hi sunt homines
ex eis coloniis quas Sulla constituit; quas ego universas civium esse optimorum et fortissimorum 25
virorum sentio, sed tamen hi sunt coloni, qui se in
insperatis repentinisque pecuniis sumptuosius insolentiusque iactarunt. Hi dum aedificant tamquam beati,
dum praediis lectis, familiis magnis, conviviis adparatis delectantur, in tantum aes alienum inciderunt, 30
ut, si salvi esse velint, Sulla sit eis ab inferis excitandus. Qui etiam non nullos agrestes homines tenues
atque egentes in eandem illam spem rapinarum
veterum impulerunt. Quos ego utrosque in eodem

35 genere praedatorum direptorumque pono, sed eos hòc
moneo : desinant furere et proscriptiones et dictaturas
cogitare. Tantus enim illorum temporum dolor in-
ustus est civitati, ut iam ista non modo homines, sed
ne pecudes quidem mihi passurae esse videantur.

fut. act. participles

*The fourth class consists of lazy ne'er-do-wells, the fifth of
desperadoes, and the sixth of effeminate rakes. The
ne'er-do-wells are too lazy to achieve anything, even by war,
while the ruffians and debauchees deserve to meet the fate
of Catiline and perish with him. It is unlikely, however,
that the last class will endure the hardships of camp life
in winter.*

X. 21. Quartum genus est sane varium et mixtum
et turbulentum, qui iam pridem premuntur, qui nunquam emergunt, qui partim inertia, partim male
gerendo negotio, partim etiam sumptibus in vetere
5 aere alieno vacillant, qui vadimoniis, iudiciis, proscriptione bonorum defatigati, permulti et ex urbe
et ex agris se in illa castra conferre dicuntur. Hosce
ego non tam milites acres quam infitiatores lentos
esse arbitror. Qui homines quam primum, si stare
10 non possunt, corruant, sed ita, ut non modo civitas,
sed ne vicini quidem proximi sentiant. Nam illud
non intellego, quam ob rem, si vivere honeste non
possunt, perire turpiter velint, aut cur minore dolore
perituros se cum multis, quam si soli pereant, arbi-
15 trentur. 22. Quintum genus est parricidarum, sicario-
rum, denique omnium facinorosorum : quos ego a
Catilina non revoco ; nam neque ab eo divelli possunt
et pereant sane in latrocinio, quoniam sunt ita multi,
ut eos carcer capere non possit. Postremum autem
20 genus est, non solum numero, verum etiam genere

ipso atque vita, quod proprium Catilinae est, de eius
dilectu, immo vero de complexu eius ac sinu, quos
pexo capillo nitidos aut imberbes aut bene barbatos
videtis, manicatis et talaribus tunicis, velis amictos,
25 non togis, quorum omnis industria vitae et vigilandi
labor in antelucanis cenis expromitur. 23. In his
gregibus omnes aleatores, omnes adulteri, omnes
impuri impudicique versantur. Hi pueri tam lepidi
ac delicati non solum amare et amari, neque saltare et
30 cantare, sed etiam sicas vibrare et spargere venena
didicerunt : qui nisi exeunt, nisi pereunt, etiam si
Catilina perierit, scitote hoc in re publica seminarium
Catilinarium futurum. Verum tamen quid sibi isti
miseri volunt? num suas secum mulierculas sunt in
35 castra ducturi? quem ad modum autem illis carere
poterunt, his praesertim iam noctibus? quo autem
pacto illi Apenninum atque illas pruinas ac nives
perferent? nisi idcirco se facilius hiemem toleraturos
putant, quod nudi in conviviis saltare didicerunt. O
40 bellum magnopere pertimescendum, cum hanc sit
habiturus Catilina scortorum cohortem praetoriam!

*The forces of the government are incomparably greater than
those of Catiline. Their morale too is higher.*

XI. 24. Instruite nunc, Quirites, contra has tam
praeclaras Catilinae copias vestra praesidia vestrosque
exercitus ; et primum gladiatori illi confecto et saucio
consules imperatoresque vestros opponite ; deinde
5 contra illam naufragorum eiectam ac debilitatam
manum, florem totius Italiae ac robur educite. Iam
vero urbes coloniarum ac municipiorum respondebunt
Catilinae tumulis silvestribus. Neque vero ceteras

copias, ornamenta, praesidia vestra, cum illius latronis
inopia atque egestate conferre debeo. 25. Sed, si, 10
omissis his rebus omnibus, quibus nos suppeditamur,
eget ille, senatu, equitibus Romanis, populo, urbe,
aerario, vectigalibus, cuncta Italia, provinciis omnibus,
exteris nationibus, si his rebus omissis, ipsas causas
quae inter se configunt contendere velimus ; ex eo 15
ipso, quam valde illi iaceant, intellegere possumus.
Ex hac enim parte pudor pugnat, illinc petulantia ;
hinc pudicitia, illinc stuprum ; hinc fides, illinc
fraudatio ; hinc pietas, illinc scelus ; hinc constantia, illinc furor ; hinc honestas, illinc turpi- 20
tudo ; hinc continentia, illinc libido : denique aequitas,
temperantia, fortitudo, prudentia, virtutes omnes,
certant cum iniquitate, cum luxuria, cum ignavia,
cum temeritate, cum vitiis omnibus : postremo, copiae
cum egestate, bona ratio cum perdita, mens sana cum 25
amentia, bona denique spes cum omnium rerum
desperatione confligit. In eius modi certamine ac
proelio nonne, si hominum studia deficiant, di ipsi
immortales cogant ab his praeclarissimis virtutibus
tot et tanta vitia superari?   30

*Citizens must guard their own homes, while Cicero will protect
the city and take every precaution. A last warning to
Catiline's supporters—'Leave the city or take the conse-
quences!'*

XII. 26. Quae cum ita sint, Quirites, vos, quem ad
modum iam antea dixi, vestra tecta vigiliis custodiis-
que defendite : mihi, ut urbi sine vestro motu ac
sine ullo tumultu satis esset praesidii, consultum atque
provisum est. Coloni omnes municipesque vestri, 5

E

certiores a me facti de hac nocturna excursione Catilinae, facile urbes suas finesque defendent. Gladiatores, quam sibi ille manum certissimam fore putavit,
quamquam animo meliore sunt quam pars patriciorum,
10 potestate tamen nostra continebuntur. Q. Metellus,
quem ego hoc prospiciens in agrum Gallicum Picenum-
que praemisi, aut opprimet hominem aut eius omnes
motus conatusque prohibebit. Reliquis autem de
rebus constituendis, maturandis, agendis iam ad
15 senatum referemus, quem vocari videtis.

27. Nunc illos, qui in urbe remanserunt atque adeo
qui contra urbis salutem omniumque vestrum in
urbe a Catilina relicti sunt, quamquam sunt hostes,
tamen, quia sunt cives, monitos etiam atque etiam
20 volo. Mea lenitas adhuc si cui solutior visa est, hoc
exspectavit, ut id quod latebat erumperet. Quod
reliquum est, iam non possum oblivisci, meam hanc
esse patriam, me horum esse consulem, mihi aut cum
his vivendum aut pro his esse moriendum. Nullus
25 est portis custos, nullus insidiator viae ; si qui exire
volunt, conivere possum ; qui vero se in urbe commoverit, cuius ego non modo factum, sed inceptum
ullum conatumve contra patriam deprehendero, sentiet
in hac urbe esse consules vigilantes, esse egregios
30 magistratus, esse fortem senatum, esse arma, esse
carcerem, quem vindicem nefariorum ac manifestorum
scelerum maiores nostri esse voluerunt.

*All will be done with the greatest order and the least disturbance.
The gods are on their side : therefore pray that they will
defend the city which they have raised to such heights of
power and world-wide dominion.*

XIII. 28. Atque haec omnia sic agentur, Quirites,
ut res maximae minimo motu, pericula summa nullo
tumultu, bellum intestinum ac domesticum, post
hominum memoriam crudelissimum ac maximum, me
5 uno togato duce et imperatore, sedetur. Quod ego
sic administrabo, Quirites, ut, si ullo modo fieri poterit,
ne improbus quidem quisquam in hac urbe poenam
sui sceleris sufferat. Sed, si vis manifestae audaciae,
si impendens patriae periculum, me necessario de hac
10 animi lenitate deduxerint, illud profecto perficiam,
quod in tanto et tam insidioso bello vix optandum
videtur, ut neque bonus intereat, paucorumque poena
vos iam omnes salvi esse possitis.

29. Quae quidem ego, neque mea prudentia neque
15 humanis consiliis fretus, polliceor vobis, Quirites ;
sed multis et non dubiis deorum immortalium signi-
ficationibus, quibus ego ducibus in hanc spem sen-
tentiamque sum ingressus : qui iam non procul, ut
quondam solebant, ab externo hoste atque longinquo,
20 sed hic praesentes suo numine atque auxilio sua
templa atque urbis tecta defendunt : quos vos,
Quirites, precari, venerari, implorare debetis, ut, quam
urbem pulcherrimam florentissimamque esse voluerunt,
hanc, omnibus hostium copiis terra marique superatis,
25 a perditissimorum civium nefario scelere defendant.

NOTES

FIRST SPEECH

CHAPTER I

Sections 1–3

Line 1. **quo usque** : **quo**, the interrogative adverb (' to what extent ') is here strengthened by **usque,** and the whole phrase =' how far '.

l. 1. **tandem.** Note this use of **tandem** with questions or commands, =' pray ', *or* ' I ask '.

l. 1. **abutere.** The following verbs show that this is future (**abutēre**). Note the 2nd sing. ending -**re** of the passive voice.

l. 2. **etiam,** ' yet ' *or* ' still ', to be taken with **quam diu.**

ll. 3–7. **nihilne . . . moverunt.** Note the effective repetition of **nihil** =' in no way '.

We may retain this repetition by translating fairly literally and rendering **nihil** by ' hasn't ' ; e.g. ' Hasn't the nightly garrison on the Palatium affected you, haven't the patrols in the city, hasn't fear of the people . . .'. Or we may turn into the passive, ' have you been in no way affected by the nightly garrison . . ., in no way by the patrols . . .'.

l. 4. **Palatii.** The Palatium or Palatine Hill, a commanding height, south-east of the Capitoline Hill, was always occupied by troops in times of emergency.

l. 5. **populi,** a good example of what is known as the objective genitive, ' fear for the people '. The name objective is given where the relation of a genitive to the noun on which it depends, is similar to that between an object and its verb.

l. 5. **bonorum.** Cicero, as a moderate conservative, naturally identifies ' good (i.e. loyal) citizens ' with the ' optimates ' or senatorial party.

37

l. 6. **hic . . . habendi senatus locus,** ' this protected place of (for) the senate to be held ', i.e. ' for holding the senate '.

Note this use of the gerundive, which in the genitive case is alternative to the use of the gerund + direct object.

A guard of **equites** (or knights) surrounded the senate. The latter met either in the Council Hall (**Curia Hostilia,** north of the **Comitium**), or in one of the temples near the **Forum.** In this case, the senate was meeting in the temple of **Jupiter Stator,** near the Sacred Way (**Via Sacra**) on the north slope of the Palatine Hill. Thus the members would be protected by the troops stationed there. At the same time, the temple was near Cicero's house.

Such precautions as these show to what extent constitutional law and order had broken down under the Republic.

l. 7. **horum,** ' of these men here '.

l. 9. **proxima . . . superiore nocte,** ' last night . . . the night before last '. The former was the night of the 7th–8th November. On the latter, Catiline held a meeting of his supporters in the house of M. Porcius Laeca, disclosed his plans, and demanded the assassination of Cicero.

ll. 9–12. **quid arbitraris.** Order for translation : **quem nostrum arbitraris ignorare quid . . .,** ' which of us, do you think, does not know . . .'.

Note **egeris, fueris, convocaveris, ceperis,** subjunctives **in** indirect question, depending on **ignorare.**

l. 12. **O tempora, o mores !,** exclamations, ' What times ! what conduct ! '

l. 14. **fit . . . particeps,** ' he becomes a partner in a public meeting ' = ' he takes part in a public meeting '.

Note that **consilium** which usually means ' counsel ', ' deliberation ' may sometimes = ' council ', ' meeting '.

l. 15. **unum quemque nostrum,** ' each one of us '.

l. 17. **si . . . vitemus,** ' should we avoid '. **vitemus,** present subjunctive, in a conditional clause of the *ideal* type. See the note on Chap. VIII, l. 1.

l. 18. **te, Catilina, duci iam pridem oportebat,** *lit.,* ' it behoved you long since, Catiline, to be led ', i.e. ' you ought long ago to have been led '.

l. 18. **iussu consulis.** In times of grave emergency, it was customary for the senate to confer unrestricted powers upon the two consuls by a special decree (**senatus consultum ultimum**). The wording of this decree is given by Cicero in Chap. II, ll. 1–2.

In this case, such authority had been given as long ago as Oct. 22nd.

l. 19. **conferri,** supply **oportebat.**

ll. 20–24. **an vero . . . perferemus.** After reading these two sentences, note that Latin prefers co-ordinate sentences without a conjunction, while English would use subordination and begin the first sentence with ' while '. This absence of a conjunction, which is common in Latin where a contrast is required, is known as asyndeton.

l. 20. **P. Scipio . . . Ti. Gracchum.** Tiberius Gracchus, a member of a distinguished and noble family, when tribune in 133 B.C., endeavoured to initiate several important reforms. In doing so, he neglected the time-honoured custom of gaining the senate's approval before putting his proposals directly before the people. Fearing that this action might establish a dangerous precedent and undermine their control, certain die-hard sections of the senate, led by P. Scipio Nasica, countenanced Tiberius' murder when he sought re-election the following year.

l. 21. **mediocriter labefactantem,** ' (when he was) somewhat weakening '—a very mild expression which is used to heighten the villainy of Catiline who is aiming at setting the whole world in flames (**orbem . . . cupientem**).

l. 22. **privatus,** ' (though) a private citizen ', i.e. he held no official position in the state.

l. 25. **quod . . .,** ' namely the fact that '.

l. 25. **C. Servilius Ahala . . . Sp. Maelium.** During a great famine at Rome in 440 B.C., Spurius Maelius, a wealthy plebeian knight, bought up corn in Etruria and distributed it free of charge to the people. He was accused by the patricians of aiming at royal power—a common charge in the early days of the Republic. A dictator was appointed and Servilius Ahala his deputy [1] slew the knight, because he refused to appear before the dictator's tribunal.

l. 27. **ista** (in agreement with **virtus**) = ' such '. Normally **iste** refers to that which concerns the Second Person rather than to facts which the speaker mentions himself.

l. 29. **senatus consultum,** i.e. the decree of October 22nd. See the note on l. 18.

l. 30. **vehemens,** neuter, in agreement with **consultum.**

l. 31. **consilium . . . auctoritas huius ordinis,** ' the advice . . . sanction of this house '.

l. 32. **desumus,** supply **rei publicae,** dative case.

CHAPTER II

Sections 4–6

lines 1–5. **L. Opimius . . . C. Gracchus . . . M. Fulvius.**
Ten years after the murder of Tiberius Gracchus, Gaius, his younger brother, was elected tribune in 123 B.C., and at once boldly embarked on a series of large-scale reforms. Unlike his brother, he definitely aimed at breaking the stranglehold which the senatorial order had over the constitution. For two years he remained unchecked. The senate, however, put up a fellow tribune to outbid Gaius Gracchus with even more generous reforms, so that owing to loss of popularity with the people, he failed to secure re-election, for the third successive year, to the tribunate. In the riots that inevitably followed, the senate declared Gaius Gracchus, and his follower M. Fulvius Flaccus, public enemies, and entrusted dictatorial power to the consul L. Opimius. As we can read in Cicero's own words, both reformers were put to death.

---

[1] Officially known as ' the master of the horse ', **magister equitum.**

l. 2. **ne quid . . . detrimenti**, ' that-not anything of harm '
=' that no harm ',—object of **caperet**. Note **detrimenti**,
partitive genitive, which is often found after neuter adjectives
denoting amount.

l. 3. **propter quasdam seditionum suspiciones**. Note the mild-
ness of the expression and compare the note on Chap. I, l. 21.

l. 4. **clarissimo patre, avo, maioribus**. Supply **natus**, or
ortus, ' sprung *or* descended from.'
His father had a distinguished career in Spain, while his
maternal grandfather was P. Scipio Africanus the elder, who
brought the Second Punic War to an end by defeating Hannibal
at the battle of Zama in N. Africa in 202 B.C.

l. 7. **num . . . remorata est**, *lit.*, ' surely death, [and] the
penalty (inflicted by) the state did not keep L. Saturninus,
tribune of the people, and C. Servilius, praetor, waiting a single
day afterwards ? ' . . .
Note : (i) **num** =' surely not ' introducing questions to
which the answer ' no ' is expected.
(ii) **ac** is explanatory and should be omitted in English.
Cicero seems to suggest that these two men must have been
expecting death for a long time, but as soon as the senate's
decree was passed, they had not to wait even a single day. In
other words, they were put to death on the same day as the
decree was passed.
Saturninus, a violent reformer without the ideals of the
Gracchi brothers, when tribune in 100 B.C. and a supporter
of the consul Marius, attempted to further the candidature for
the consulship of his friend Glaucia, a man of ambitions similar
to his own, by murdering his rival at the elections. In reply,
the senate called on the consuls to safeguard the state. Saturninus, Glaucia, and their supporters were arrested, and eventually lost their lives at the hands of the people.

l. 10. **vicesimum . . . patimur**. ' (It is) now the 20th day
(that) we have allowed . . .'.
Note : the present tense of **patimur**, customary in Latin
with phrases like **iam, iam pridem**.[1] Cf. the French *je vous*

[1] Where the action is continued into present time.

attends depuis longtemps : ' I have been waiting for you a
long time '.

The chronology is not quite correct. Actually it was
eighteen days since the senate passed its decree on the 22nd of
October.

l. 11. **horum,** ' of these men here ' =' of the senate '.

l. 14. **quo ex . . . convenit,** ' in accordance with which decree
it is fitting that you (=you might well) have been put to death
immediately '.

l. 16. **patres conscripti,** ' enrolled fathers ', i.e. ' the senators '.

l. 20. **in Etruriae faucibus,** near the modern Fiesole, about
five miles from Florence. This pass lies on a western spur of
the Apennines and gives access northwards into the Lombardy
Plain, southwards into Etruria (modern Tuscany).

l. 23. **adeo,** ' actually '.

l. 24. **molientem,** agrees with **imperatorem ducemque** and
has for its object **intestinam aliquam perniciem.**

l. 26. **credo,** parenthetical (i.e. it is outside the structure
of the rest of the sentence and therefore has no influence
on it).

l. 26. **erit verendum mihi,** ' it will have-to-be-feared by me ',
i.e. ' I shall have to fear '.

Note that in the nominative,[1] the gerundive expresses
' ought ', ' must ', ' should '. The neuter is always used with
intransitive verbs.

l. 26. **ne . . . dicat,** *lit.,* ' not that all loyal men (will say)
that this has been done by me too late rather than anyone
will say that it has been done too cruelly.'

As the whole sentence is ironic, we may translate, ' I shall
have to fear, I suppose, not that all loyal men will say I have
acted too late but that someone will say that I have been
too cruel.'

l. 28. **hoc,** object of **faciam,** l. 30, and antecedent of the
following **quod.**

---

[1] and accusative in Oratio Obliqua.

l. 32. qui . . . fateatur, ' as to admit '. The subjunctive is consecutive for qui = ut is, ' that he '.

l. 32. quam, ' as '.

l. 33. quisquam, ' anyone at all '.

l. 33. qui . . . audeat. See the note on l. 32 above.

l. 34. ut vivis, ' as indeed you do live '.

l. 36. te . . . non sentientem, ' you not perceiving ' (object of speculabuntur atque custodient) = ' you without your knowing '.

CHAPTER III

Sections 6–8

line 3. parietibus. Note : (1) murus, general term for ' a wall ', (ii) moenia, -ium, n., pl., ' city walls ', (iii) paries, -etis, m., ' wall of a house '.

l. 4. coniurationis, ' of the conspiracy ' = ' of the conspirators '.

Note that Latin sometimes uses an abstract noun (conspiracy), where we would prefer the concrete (conspirators).

l. 5. mihi crede, ' take my advice '.

l. 7. luce, ablative of comparison.

l. 8. licet recognoscas, ' you may review '.

l. 8. meministine me . . . dicere, ' do you remember my saying '.

Memini, ' I remember ', is perfect in form, present in meaning. Similar is odi, ' I hate '.

l. 8. ante diem XII Kalendas Novembres, ' on October 21st '.

l. 9. fore . . . administrum tuae. Order for translation : C. Manlium, satellitem atque administrum tuae audaciae fore in armis certo die qui (dies) esset futurus ante diem VI Kalendas Novembres.

l. 10. futurus esset, subjunctive because it is in a subordinate clause in indirect statement.

l. 10. ante diem VI Kalendas Novembres, October 27th.

l. 11. **C. Manlium.** Gaius Manlius had been a centurion in the army of the Roman general Sulla. As a man of considerable military experience, he had been appointed by Catiline as leader of the uprising in Etruria.

l. 14. **verum,** but.

l. 14. **multo magis . . . admirandum,** ' (by) much more remarkable '. Note **multo,** ablative of the measure of difference, found with comparatives.

l. 15. **ego idem,** ' I likewise ' or ' I also '.

l. 15. **caedem . . . contulisse . . . Novembres,** ' that you had fixed the slaughter of the nobles for the 28th October '.

l. 17. **tum cum,** ' at a time when '.

l. 17. **Roma,** ablative ; to be taken with **profugerunt.**

l. 18. **non tam sui conservandi . . . reprimendorum causa.**

Sui conservandi causa, ' for the sake of themselves to-be-saved =' for the sake of saving themselves '. Similarly **tuorum . . . causa.**

Note : (i) **causa,** ' for the sake of ', follows its case (genitive), (ii) the gerundive construction, which, in the genitive, is an alternative expression to the gerund with a direct object.

Finally notice how Cicero's expression here suggests that many aristocrats had left Rome merely to save their own skins. In so doing, however, they had foiled Catiline's plans by placing themselves out of his reach. Cicero's audience would appreciate this indirect censure.

l. 21. **commovere te . . . non potuisse,** ' could not have moved '.

l. 22. **discessu ceterorum,** ' on the departure of the rest '.

l. 22. **nostra . . . caede,** ' with our (=my) murder '.

l. 23. **remansissemus.** The subjunctive is similar to that in l. 10. 1st plural here =1st singular.

l. 23. **esse =fore.**

l. 24. **cum,** ' although '. In this concessive meaning, **cum** is always followed by the subjunctive mood.

l. 24. **Praeneste,** acc., object of **occupaturum.** Praeneste (mod. Palestrina) is situated on a hill 20 miles south-east of Rome and is a place of great strategical importance.

l. 27. **custodiis, vigiliis.** Note that Latin uses abstract nouns in the plural with a concrete meaning. E.g. **amicitiae** = ' friends '.   So **custodiae** =' sentinels ', **vigiliae** =' patrols '.

l. 28. **quod . . . sentiam,** *lit.*, ' which I do not, not-only hear but also see and plainly realise '.   The first **non** negatives the whole of the rest of the sentence.

Finally note that the subjunctives in the **quod** clauses are consecutive, because **quod** =**tale ut,** ' of such a kind that '.

CHAPTER IV

Sections 8–10

line 1. **tandem,** either ' pray ', ' I ask ', cf. Chap. I, l. 1, or ' however ', ' still '.   If the latter, Cicero means to remove any further doubts as to the completeness of his knowledge.

l. 1. **noctem illam superiorem.** See the note on Chap. I, l. 9.

l. 2. **iam intelleges.** Supply ' and ' before these two words.

l. 2. **multo . . . acrius.** For the abl. **multo,** see the note on Chap. III, l. 14.   **acrius,** comparative adverb (**acriter**).

l. 3. **ad,** ' with a view to '.

l. 3. **dico,** ' I assert '.

l. 4. **priore nocte** =**superiore nocte** =' the night before last '.

l. 4. **inter falcarios,** ' in the sickle-makers' street '.

l. 4. **non agam obscure,** *lit.*, ' I shall not deal (with you) obscurely ' =' I shall deal with you plainly '.

l. 5. **eodem,** *lit.*, ' *to* the same place '.   Here we would say ' *at* the same place '.

l. 6. **sceleris,** ' recklessness ', the usual meaning of the word, when coupled with abstract nouns. There are many more instances of this meaning in Books I and II.

l. 8. **tecum una ; una** is an adverb.   ' Together with you '.

l. 9. **ubinam gentium sumus ?** ' where in the world are we? '.
Note : (i) **ubi** strengthened by **nam,** (ii) **gentium,** partitive
genitive. This genitive stands for the *whole* to which a *part*
belongs, and is used particularly with nouns and neuter
adjectives denoting quantity and number.

l. 12. **in hoc . . . consilio,** ' in this most venerable and influ-
ential advisory council in the world '.

l. 13. **de nostro omnium interitu,** *lit.,* ' about our destruction
of all ' = ' about the destruction of us all '. Note that the
genitive **omnium** agrees with the genitive understood from
and implied in the possessive adjective **nostro.**

l. 13. **qui . . . cogitent,** ' (men so wicked) as to devise '.
cogitent, consecutive subjunctive because **qui = tales ut ei.**

l. 14. **adeo,** ' actually '.

l. 15. **sententiam rogo,** ' I ask (them) their opinion '.
In a debate in the senate, the presiding magistrate (either
consul or tribune) called on the members present to express
their opinion, beginning with the senior members.

l. 16. **quos . . . vulnero :** **eos** is the antecedent of **quos.**

l. 16. **nondum voce vulnero.** Cicero means that he has not
yet attacked them by mentioning them by name or by bringing
a formal charge against them.

l. 17. **igitur,** refers back to **num negare audes,** l. 6, which,
it is obvious, Catiline has left unanswered. *Therefore,* he was
present at Laeca's house.

l. 18. **quo . . . placeret,** *lit.,* ' where it was pleasing that each
man was to go ' = ' where each man was to go '.

l. 19. **quos relinqueres, . . . educeres,** ' whom to leave behind,
. . . whom to take . . .'.
relinqueres, educeres are good examples of what is known
as the indirect deliberative subjunctive. The direct form
would be **quos relinquam . . . educam ?** ' whom am I to leave
behind, whom am I to lead ? '

l. 22. **paulum . . . morae,** ' a little (of) delay '.
For the genitive, see the note on l. 9 in this chapter.

l. 23. **viverem.** Note the subjunctive ; subordinate clause in indirect speech.

l. 23. **duo equites.** These men were C. Cornelius and L. Vargunteius. The knights (**equites**) ranked as a class in political importance next to the senate, and, at this time, included most of the business men such as bankers, rich merchants, and capitalists.

In politics, they sometimes sided with the senatorial party, and sometimes with the popular party and their leaders. It was Cicero's great ambition to unite the senatorial and equestrian classes to form the basis of a strong, stable government.

l. 24. **qui . . . liberarent . . . pollicerentur.** Note the subjunctive mood, expressing purpose.

l. 24. **paulo ante lucem ;** for the ablative **paulo,** see the note on Chap. III, l. 14.

l. 25. **interfecturos esse.** Note that verbs of *hoping, promising, threatening, swearing* regularly take acc. and future infinitive. E.g. ' I promise to come ', **polliceor me venturum esse.**

l. 26. **Haec ego . . . comperi.** English idiom would probably reverse the role of main clause and ablative absolute, and make the latter the main clause, the former subordinate. ' Scarcely had your meeting broken up when *I* discovered all these facts '.

l. 29. **salutatum,** accusative of the supine, expressing purpose, used most commonly after verbs of sending.

We might translate **salutatum mane** by ' to pay an early morning call ', *lit.,* ' to greet early '.

At this time in Rome, distinguished men received regular early morning visits from humble friends and those anxious for advancement, who called to pay their respects, and, if necessary, dance attendance upon their patron.

In earlier times, the relation of client to patron resembled that of vassal to chief, but, in the first century B.C. and later, this relationship tended to be degraded.

l. 29. **cum,** ' since '.

l. 31. **id temporis,** ' at that time '. Note : (i) **temporis,** partitive genitive, (ii) **id,** accusative of extent in time (adverbial accusative).

CHAPTER V

Sections 10–13

Line 1. **cum,** ' since '. In this meaning, **cum** is always followed by the subjunctive mood.

l. 2. **egredere,** imperative (2nd sing.) of **egredior.**

l. 2. **aliquando,** ' at last '.

l. 3. **nimium diu . . . desiderant.** For the tense, see the note on Chap. II, l. 10.

l. 5. **si minus,** supply **omnes,** ' or if not all '.

l. 5. **magno metu,** a good example of the ablative of separation.

l. 6. **dum modo,** ' provided only '. In this meaning, **dum** is always followed by the subjunctive mood.

l. 8. **non feram, non patiar, non sinam.** Latin often uses synonymous[1] verbs to express a thought forcibly. English uses verb and adverb. E.g. ' I strongly beg of you ', becomes in Latin **te oro atque obsecro** . . .

In this passage Cicero wishes to say, ' I will not endure it under any circumstances '. Perhaps we may render, ' I cannot, I will not, I shall not endure it ' (Wilkins).

l. 8. **magna . . . habenda est . . . gratia,** ' deep gratitude is to be felt ', i.e. ' we should feel deep gratitude '.

For the gerundive in the nominative expressing ' ought ', ' must ', ' should ' see also Chap. II, l. 26. Note that the gerundive in Latin is passive, but that it is often best rendered into English by the active voice.

l. 9. **huic ipsi Iovi Statori.** Cicero points to the statue of the god in whose temple the senate is holding its session.

---

[1] Of the same meaning.

l. 10. **antiquissimo,** because the temple was believed to have been dedicated by Romulus, the legendary founder of Rome (*c.* 753 B.C.).

l. 12. **non est . . . rei publicae,** ' the supreme safety of the state is not to-be-risked repeatedly in the person of one man '. More freely : ' it must not repeatedly be one person's fault that the supreme safety of the state be endangered .'

l. 14. **quam,** ' as '.

l. 14. **consuli designato.** Cicero was consul elect in the winter of 64–63 B.C. Consuls entered office on the 1st March and were usually elected in the July previous by the comitia centuriata.

l. 16. **proximis comitiis consularibus,** ' at the last consular elections '. The comitia centuriata, or ' assembly by hun- dreds ', was originally an organisation of the citizens of Rome for military mobilisation. Later it became the most important assembly of the people, elected the higher magistrates, decided the vital questions of war or peace, and acted as a court of appeal, while whatever measures it accepted, became binding as laws on all citizens.

The comitia centuriata met in the Campus Martius (or ' Plain of Mars '), the north-west part of the level ground which lay in a bend of the Tiber outside the walls of Rome.

l. 17. **in campo.** See the previous note.

l. 19. **nullo . . . concitato,** *lit.,* ' no alarm having been aroused on the part of the state ' =' without any official mobili- sation of troops '.

l. 20. **per me,** ' by myself '.

l. 21. **perniciem meam . . . coniunctam.** Note Cicero's vanity. He was excessively proud of his achievements during this consulship when he crushed with promptitude and vigour the conspiracy of Catiline, and, in later years never tired of referring to them. There is no doubt that he really felt that he deserved the title of **Pater Patriae** which was conferred upon him.

l. 26. **quare quoniam . . . audeo.** Order for translation :

quare quoniam nondum audeo facere quod est primum **et
quod est proprium** huius imperii disciplinaeque maiorum.

l. 26. **quod est primum,** ' what would be the first thing (to
do) '. Latin sometimes says ' is ' where we use ' would be '.

l. 27. **disciplinaeque maiorum,** ' and the best traditions of
our ancestors '. **disciplinae,** [like **huius imperii.**] gen., depending
on **proprium.**

l. 29. **ad severitatem,** ' as regards severity '.
Similarly **ad communem salutem.**

l. 30. **si . . . iussero.** Note the future-perfect in Latin,
where we use the present. Latin is more precise and exact
in its use of tenses in subordinate clauses. It is obvious that
the action of the ' if ' clause must precede that of the main
clause (apodosis). Similarly **exieris** in l. 32.

l. 32. **te iam dudum hortor.** For the present tense (=our
perfect), see the note on Chap. II, l. 10.

l. 32. **tuorum . . . rei publicae,** *lit.*, ' the great and dangerous
refuse of the state (consisting) of your companions '. Translate
' your many dangerous companions, the refuse of the state '.
sentina literally means ' bilge-water '.

l. 34. **dubitas . . . facere.** Note that **dubito** (1) when followed by the infinitive means ' hesitate '.

l. 35. **faciebas,** ' were ready to do '. The imperfect tense
in Latin is often used of *attempted, intended* or *expected* actions.

CHAPTER VI

Sections 13–16

Line 1. **quod . . . possit.** Note the consecutive subjunctive,
quod = tale ut id. This subjunctive is common in relative
clauses where the antecedent consists of a word like **idoneus,
aptus, dignus,** etc., or where the antecedent is indefinite,
especially after negatives.

In this case, the question ' What is there? ' is negative in
character, because it suggests that ' there is nothing '. Cf. also
metuat, l. 4, **oderit,** l. 4.

l. 3. **coniurationem** = ' band of conspirators '. Note that while Latin on the whole prefers concrete terms to abstract ones, it sometimes uses abstract where English has concrete.

l. 4. **oderit.** Like **memini,** ' I remember ', **odi,** ' I hate ' is *perfect* in form, *present* in meaning.

l. 4. **quae nota,** etc. Cicero now proclaims the scandals and vices of Catiline's private life. Such an attack to-day would be considered irrelevant or, if permitted at all, bad taste, in the Houses of Parliament or a jury-court, or even on a public platform. But in Greek and Roman times, such mud-slinging was customary and, indeed, expected.

l. 4. **domesticae turpitudinis.** This phrase refers to the scandals of his home life. See later.

l. 5. **privatarum rerum dedecus.** This phrase points to the scandal of his private life outside his own immediate family circle.

l. 8. **cui tu adulescentulo . . . non . . . ferrum . . . facem praetulisti?** ' Before what weak youth . . . did you not carry either the sword for . . . or the torch for . . .?

adulescentulo ; note that diminutives imply either endearment (cf. **lectulo,** Chap. IV, l. 25, ' my *comfortable* bed ') or contempt, as here.

facem praetulisti. The metaphor is taken from the practice of slaves who used to run before their masters at night with a lighted torch, to light them home.

l. 12. **novis nuptiis,** dative case.

l. 12. **domum vacuefecisses.** Note the language Cicero uses to charge Catiline with murdering his first wife. No other Roman author corroborates this accusation.

l. 13. **alio incredibili scelere.** Sallust (Roman historian [1] who wrote a monograph on Catiline) states that Catiline fell in love with a beautiful but profligate woman. As, however, she objected to marrying him because he had a grown-up son, Catiline removed him by poisoning.

In another passage in the same work, Sallust admits that

---

[1] A contemporary of Cicero.

several people believed such charges to have been invented by those who hoped to decrease the unpopularity of Cicero which arose as a result of the execution of the conspirators.

l. 14. **ne,** ' lest '.

l. 16. **non vindicata esse.** Cicero intends his hearers to take this as a sign of evil days, viz. that such a horrid crime as he has laid to Catiline's charge should go unpunished. On the other hand, the fact that Catiline was not brought to trial may suggest that there was in reality very little evidence in support of Cicero's charge. See also the preceding note.

l. 16. **ruinas,** ' the downfall ' or ' collapse '. For the plural, see the note on Chap. III, l. 27.

l. 17. **omnes.** In Latin, adjectives, especially superlatives, are often transferred from the antecedent into the relative clause and made to agree with the relative pronoun. So here. Translate **omnes** by ' utter ' or ' complete ', and take it with the antecedent **ruinas.**

l. 17. **proximis Idibus,** ' at the next Ides '. The Romans used three fixed days in expressing dates, the Kalends (1st of the month), the Nones (5th or 7th [1] of the month) and the Ides (always 8 days later than the Nones). Intervening dates between these fixed days were expressed by such and such [2] a day before the next fixed day, e.g. **ante diem XII Kalendas Novembres,** Chap. III, l. 8, and other examples.

These fixed days were the ' settling-days ' at Rome, and Cicero points out that at the next Ides when Catiline's conspiracy will be recognised as a failure, his creditors will immediately call in the money they have lent him. His bankruptcy will follow on the following Kalends, the usual day of payment.

l. 18. **quae non . . . pertinent.** Note **pertinere ad,** ' to concern '.

l. 18. **privatam ignominiam vitiorum tuorum,** ' the personal disgrace, (the result) of your vices '.

l. 20. **difficultatem,** ' money difficulties '.

---

[1] In March, July, October, May.
[2] Inclusive reckoning must be used.

l. 20. **ad summam rem publicam,** ' the supreme danger of the state '.

l. 21. **omnium nostrum,** ' of us all '. **nostrum,** genitive plural of **nos.**

l. 23. **spiritus,** ' breath ', ' air '.

l. 23. **cum,** ' when '.

l. 24. **pridie Kalendas Ianuarias,** *lit.*, ' the day before the 1st of January ' =' Dec. 31st '. The year was 66 B.C.

This is the usual way of expressing the date of a day before a fixed date.

Cicero is referring to the First Catilinarian Conspiracy, for which see the Introduction, pp. xv, xvi.

l. 25. **Lepido et Tullo consulibus,** ' Lepidus and Tullus consuls ' =' in the consulship of L. and T.'. Cf. **me duce,** ' under my leadership '. The construction is ablative absolute.

l. 26. **in comitio.** The comitium was a paved area of about 80 yards square on the north-west side of the Forum. In the comitium were held (in early times) the assemblies of the Roman people for purposes other than elections.

l. 26. **cum telo,** ' with a weapon (in your hand) '.

l. 26. **manum,** ' band ' or ' force '.

l. 26. **consulum . . . causa,** *lit.*, ' for the sake of the consuls and leading men of the state to be killed ' =' for the sake of killing the consuls ', etc.

Note **causa** =' for the sake of ', always *follows* its case.

l. 27. **sceleri ac furori tuo,** dative, dependent on **obstitisse** which takes that case.

l. 28. **mentem,** ' reflection '.

l. 28. **timorem tuum,** ' fear on your part '.

l. 29. **fortunam.** It is said that Catiline's plot failed because he gave the signal too soon.

l. 30. **neque . . . postea. Neque** qualifies the whole sentence. So the second half literally runs : ' nor (were) not-many (offences) later committed (by you) =' and many offences were later . . .'.

l. 33. **petitiones**, ' thrusts ', a technical term taken from the gladiatorial school, where ' cut ' and ' thrust ' tactics were taught. Cicero continues the metaphor in the next line.

l. 34. **parva . . . corpore**, ' by a mere swerve and (turn of) the body, as they say '.

l. 38. **quae . . . defigere**. Note : (i) **quae**, co-ordinating relative =' and . . . this ', agreeing with **sica** (understood), subject of **devota sit**. (ii) **quibus . . . sacris . . . sit,** indirect question, dependent on **nescio**.

Order for translation : **nescio quidem quibus sacris quae** (=this) **(sica) initiata ac devota sit abs te quod,** etc.

Cicero is referring to the practice of assassins (common in antiquity), dedicating to a god the weapons by which they had successfully perpetrated some murder.

CHAPTER VII

Sections 16–18

Line 3. **quo debeo,** ' by which I ought (to be influenced)'.

l. 3. **nulla** =' in no way '.

l. 6. **post hominum memoriam** =' in (=within) the recollec-tion of man '.

l. 6. **vocis . . . contumeliam,** ' the contempt of the voice ' = ' the contempt of their words ' or ' their spoken contempt '.

l. 7. **gravissimo . . . taciturnitatis,** ' by the very heavy judgment of their silence ' =' by the weight of their silent judgment '.

l. 8. **quid, quod . . .,** *lit.,* ' what (shall we say of the fact) that '.

l. 10. **tibi,** dative of the person interested, ' in your mind '. This dative is very similar to the dative of the agent, found with the gerundive expressing ' ought ', ' must ', ' should '. Cf. **tibi** in the following note.

l. 12. **quo tandem . . . putas,** ' with what feelings, pray, do you think this is to be endured by you? ' Note once again that the gerundive in the nominative and accusative in indirect speech as here, expresses ' ought ', ' must ', ' should '. It is better to translate the gerundive in the active and personally, i.e. ' you should endure this '.

l. 13. **mehercule**, ' by Hercules '. This expression is probably a shortened form of **me, Hercules, iuves**, ' mayest thou, O Hercules, help me.'

l. 13. **si . . . metuerent, . . . putarem.** A good example of a conditional clause, unreal in present time. Note the imperfect subjunctive in both protasis and apodosis. ' If my slaves feared me . . . , I should think '.

l. 14. **ut . . . metuunt. ut** with the indicative means ' as ', or ' when ' : it means ' as ' here.

l. 15. **domum . . . relinquendam** (esse), ' my house is to be left by me ' =' I ought to leave my house '. See the note on l. 12 above.

l. 16. **urbem.** Supply **relinquendam esse.**

l. 16. **iniuria,** ' unjustly '.

l. 19. **conspici.** Parse carefully.

l. 19. **conscientia scelerum tuorum,** ' in the consciousness of your crimes ' =' in your guilty conscience '.

l. 20. **odium omnium,** ' the hatred of all ' =' the universal hatred '.

l. 21. **dubitas,** ' do you hesitate? '

l. 21. **quorum . . . vitare.** Translate **vitare adspectum praesentiamque eorum** first, and note the position of the antecedent of **quorum.**

l. 23. **si . . . timerent, . . . posses, . . . concederes.** See the note on l. 13 above.

Odissent. Remember that **odi,** ' I hate ' is perfect in form, but present in meaning. Hence **odissent** is equivalent to the imperfect subjunctive.

l. 23. **tui,** take with **parentes,** ' your own parents '.

l. 25. **nunc,** ' but as it is '.

l. 26. **iam diu . . . iudicat,** ' has long been of the opinion '. For the tense, see the note on Chap. II, l. 10.

l. 27. **nihil te nisi . . . cogitare,** ' that you think of nothing except . . . '.

l. 27. **de parricidio suo.** Parricide strictly means ' the murder of one's parents ', but it may also include treason against one's country. The word is very apt here because Cicero is talking of his country as the common parent of all.

Translate by ' of her destruction '.

l. 28. **verebere = vereberis,** 2nd sing. future indicative. Similarly **sequere,** ' abide by ' or ' bow to '.

l. 29. **quae,** co-ordinating relative. ' And she '.

l. 30. **tacita loquitur,** ' silently pleads (with you) '. Note the oxymoron or combining in one expression two terms that are ordinarily contradictory and whose exceptional coincidence is therefore arresting, e.g., ' a cheerful pessimist '.[1]

l. 31. **aliquot annis,** ' for several years '. Note that with negative phrases, the ablative, not the accusative, is used for *duration of time.*

l. 32. **tibi uni,** ' in your case alone ', dative of the *person interested.*

l. 32. **multorum civium neces.** A reference to the part Catiline took in the Sullan proscriptions.

l. 33. **sociorum,** ' of allies ' = ' of the provincials '.

In 67 B.C. Catiline had been propraetor of Africa and prosecuted for extortion and misgovernment. In spite of strong evidence, he was acquitted.

l. 34. **ad neglegendas leges . . . perfringendasque,** ' for the laws and courts to-be-disregarded but also to-be-overthrown and destroyed '.

Note that in the accusative case after the preposition **ad,** Latin prefers the gerundive construction for the English gerund with direct object. So here we would say, ' for disregarding the law and courts but also for overthrowing and destroying them '.

l. 36. **Superiora illa,** neuter plural, object of **tuli ;** ' your former actions '.

[1] *Modern English Usage,* Fowler.

l. 36. **ferenda . . . fuerunt.** See the note on l. 12 above.

l. 37. **nunc vero me . . . non est ferendum.** Note : (i) **me . . . unum te ; quidquid . . . timeri ; nullum . . . abhorreat,** are in the accusative and infinitive construction dependent on **non est ferendum** which should be translated first.

l. 37. **totam,** in agreement with **me,** ' wholly '. It is feminine, because, it will be remembered, the *motherland* is addressing Catiline.

l. 38. **quidquid increpuerit,** *lit.,* ' (that) whatever has been noised abroad ' =' at every little rumour '.
Increpuerit is perfect subjunctive.

l. 39. **nullum . . . posse :** order for translation : **nullum consilium posse videri iniri contra me.**

l. 40. **abhorreat.** Explain the subjunctive.

CHAPTER VIII

Sections 19–21

Line 1. **si . . . loquatur, . . . debeat, . . . possit.** A good example of an ideal conditional clause, where the supposition is more or less fanciful, ' Should your country speak . . ., should she not obtain . . .'. Note the present subjunctive in both protasis and apodosis.

l. 3. **quid, quod . . .** See the note on Chap. VII, l. 8.

l. 3. **in custodiam.** A week or two before Cicero delivered this speech, Catiline had been impeached on a charge of causing revolution and riots. When a citizen was on a criminal charge, he either gave bail for his appearance in court, or was entrusted to the custody of some distinguished citizen. In this case, to throw off all suspicion and to conceal his real plans as long as possible, Catiline voluntarily offered to place himself in the custody of various distinguished men. He approached Manius Lepidus who had been consul in 66 B.C., Memmius the praetor and even Cicero himself. They all refused to have such a charge on their hands.

l. 4. **vitandae suspicionis causa.** For **causa** and the gerundive construction, read the note on Chap. III, l. 18.

l. 4. **ad = apud.** French *chez*.

l. 5. **receptus,** perf. part. passive of **recipio,** ' (when you were) not received '.

l. 8. **me . . . tecum,** ' (namely) that I could in no way be safe . . .'.

l. 9. **qui . . . essem, quod . . . contineremur.** Note : (i) **qui** + subj. = **cum ego** (causal), ' since I was . . .'. (ii) **quod** causal, with the subjunctive, because the clause is subordinate in oratio obliqua.

l. 11. **virum optimum, M. Metellum,** sarcastic ; ' that fine fellow Marcus Metellus '.

l. 13. **diligentissimum . . ., sagacissimum, . . . fortissimum,** sarcastic again : **fortissimum,** ' very resolute '.

Nothing beyond what is said here is known about Marcus Metellus, but the presence of Catiline at the meeting at Laeca's house during his supposed voluntary ' detention ' on bail at the house of Marcus Metellus shows the real value of his ' bail '.

l. 15. **quam longe . . . debere,** ' how far does he seem he ought to be away from . . .'. Latin uses **videor,** ' I seem ' *personally,* whereas we prefer to use it *impersonally.* So here we should say, ' how far does it seem that he should be free from . . .'.

l. 15. **a carcere atque a vinculis ;** a reference to the State Prison which was used for detention and execution, not for penal servitude. See the note on l. 3 above.

l. 16. **qui . . . iudicarit,** ' in as much as he judged . . .'.

Note again that **qui** (= **cum is,** causal) is followed by the subjunctive mood.

iudicarit is a shortened form of **iudicaverit.** In verb forms containing the letter ' v ', that consonant and the following vowel often disappear.

custodia, ablative after **dignum.** The reference is to the type of bail or detention described in the note on l. 3 above.

l. 18. **cum,** ' since '.

l. 18. **dubitas,** ' do you hesitate? '.

l. 18. **emori aequo animo.** Cicero now suggests that if Catiline cannot face the death which he deserves either by execution or suicide, he should at any rate go into voluntary exile.

l. 20. **iustis debitisque,** ' just and due ' = ' justly due '.

l. 21. **refer . . . ad senatum,** ' put it to the senate '.

l. 22. **hic ordo,** ' this House '. Catiline probably challenged Cicero to put the matter to an open vote, because he knew the senate would shrink from openly condemning him. Cicero, however, refuses to do so, because the senate had no constitutional power to pass sentence on any citizen.

l. 25. **faciam . . . intellegas,** ' I shall make you realise '.

l. 26. **metu,** ablative of separation.

l. 27. **vocem,** ' word '.

l. 27. **proficiscere,** parse carefully. After this word, there is a short pause : then, as the senate remains silent, Cicero continues with, **quid est . . .**

l. 28. **ecquid,** neuter of **ecquis** (' is there anyone who? '), is an adverbial accusative and merely emphasises the two following questions.

l. 29. **patiuntur,** ' they suffer it ' = ' they approve *or* acquiesce '.

l. 30. **auctoritatem,** ' the expressed request '.

l. 30. **loquentium,** ' of them speaking ' = ' of their speech ' = ' of their words '. With **auctoritatem,** we may translate : ' a request expressed in words '.

l. 30. **voluntatem tacitorum,** ' silent expression of their will ' ; *lit.,* ' the will of them silent '.

l. 32. **P. Sestio.** Publius Sestius was quaestor at this time. Six years later he actively supported the return of Cicero from exile.

l. 33. **M. Marcello.** Marcellus was destined to become consul in 51 B.C., and a fierce opponent of Caesar. On being pardoned and recalled from exile in 46 B.C., he was murdered by one of his own attendants.

l. 33. **si . . . dixissem . . . intulisset.** Note the pluperfect subjunctive in both protasis and apodosis in this conditional clause (unreal in past time) ; ' if I had said . . . the senate would have laid '.

l. 34. **vim et manus,** hendiadys, ' violent hands '.

l. 36. **cum tacent, clamant.** For the oxymoron, see the note on Chap. VII, l. 30. **cum,** ' in that '.

l. 37. **auctoritas . . . cara,** a sarcastic reference to Section 20 where Catiline alleged that he was prepared to go into voluntary exile, if such was the senate's will.

l. 38. **vita vilissima,** English says ' lives '.

l. 38. **equites Romani.** Cicero points to the members of the equestrian order who could be seen standing in front of the temple where the senate was in session. When the House was sitting, the doors were always left open.

For the position of the equites in Roman society, see the note on Chap. IV, l. 23.

l. 39. **ceteri fortissimi cives, i.e.** those citizens who belonged neither to the senatorial nor to the equestrian order. Cicero, in particular, and Latin, in general, is very fond of superlative adjectives, where we should be satisfied with the positive form.

l. 41. **paulo ante.** Note the ablative of the measure of difference. Cicero is referring either to when Catiline entered the senate or to interruptions during his own speech.

l. 42. **iam diu . . . contineo.** For the tense (present where we use the perfect), see the note on Chap. II, l. 10.

l. 43. **eosdem,** the antecedent of **quorum,** l. 42.

l. 44. **haec,** ' this scene ', i.e. the city of Rome ; object of **relinquentem.**

l. 45. **prosequantur.** When a citizen went into voluntary exile, he was usually escorted out of the city by his relatives and friends. Cicero, in making a sarcastic reference to this custom, suggests that Catiline's escort will consist of men who will be glad to see him go.

CHAPTER IX

Sections 22–24

Line 1. **te . . . frangat**, *lit.*, ' that anything may break you '
=' could anything break down your resolution '.

l. 3. **meditere** =**mediteris**, 2nd person sing. pres. subj. of **meditor**.

l. 4. **duint**, an old form of the 3rd person plur. pres. subj. of **do**. Note that **utinam** + the present subj. expresses a wish for the future.

l. 6. **nobis** =**mihi**, dative, dependent on **impendeat**.

l. 6. **si minus in praesens tempus**, ' if not for the present '.

l. 7. **recenti . . . tuorum**, ablative absolute, ' while the memory of your crimes is still fresh '.

l. 8. **est tanti**, ' it is worth-while '. With this sentence, supply from the preceding sentence **invidiam istam mihi impendere**.

l. 8. **dum modo**, ' provided only '.

l. 11. **temporibus rei publicae**, ' the needs of the state '.

l. 12. **est postulandum**. For the nominative of the gerundive, see the note on Chap. VII, l. 12.

l. 12. **neque is es ut . . .**, *lit.*, ' you are not such a man that shame has ever called you back from disgrace or . . .'. The consecutive clause would be better in the passive in English : ' you are not the man to be called back from disgrace by shame ', etc.

l. 15. **mihi . . . tuo**, ' against me, your personal enemy as you assert '.

l. 16. **vis**, from **volo**.

l. 17. **sermones hominum**, ' the talk of men ' =' what men will say '.

l. 20. **importuna**, ' savage '.

l. 23. **impio**, ' impious ', because he is acting against his own fatherland.

l. 23. **ut isse videaris,** ' that you may seem to have gone '.
Note the personal construction with **videor.** English prefers
to say, ' that it may seem that you have gone '.

l. 25. **a quo sciam esse praemissos, qui . . . praestolarentur,**
lit., ' by whom I know (men) have been sent ahead to wait '.
Sciam, subjunctive after **qui** causal =' since by you ' (**cum a te**).
Translate, ' since I know you have sent ahead men to wait '.
qui . . . praestolarentur ; the subjunctive is due to **qui** (final).

l. 26. **Forum Aurelium,** the modern Montalto, about fifty
miles north of Rome on the great north road, called the Via
Aurelia.

l. 27. **cui = cum tibi.** See the note above, l. 25. **tibi,** dative
of the person interested.

l. 28. **a quo . . . praemissam.** Order for translation : **a quo**
sciam (causal) **illam aquilam argenteam esse praemissam**
quam confido . . . futuram . . .

l. 28. **quam . . . futuram,** in parenthesis.

l. 28. **aquilam illam.** According to the Roman historian
and contemporary of Cicero and Catiline, Sallust, this eagle
was said to have belonged to the famous Roman general
Marius, who repelled two serious Gallic invasions of Italy forty
years before the date of this speech, i.e. in 101 B.C.
Marius introduced many reforms in the Roman army and
was the first to use the eagle as a standard.

l. 30. **sacrarium scelerum,** ' a shrine of crime '. There is a
reference here to the **sacrarium** in the Roman military camp, a
spot near the general's tent (**praetorium**) where the eagles were
kept. The **sacrarium** was considered sacred.

l. 31. **tu ut . . . possis,** ' (to think) that you can any longer
go without that (eagle) '. Note that **carere** is followed by the
ablative case.

l. 33. **a cuius altaribus,** ' and from its altar '. Classical
Latin uses **altaria** only in the plural.

CHAPTER X

Sections 25–27

Line 1. **quo,** *lit.,* ' whither '. Translate ' (to that place) where '.

l. 3. **haec res,** ' this conduct (of yours) ' : i.e. making war upon your country.

l. 3. **quandam incredibilem voluptatem,** ' a kind of joy beyond belief '.

l. 5. **voluntas,** ' your own inclination '.

l. 6. **non modo . . . sed ne quidem. non modo**=**non modo non,** as it often does when the two negative phrases have a verb in common. The negative strengthens the previous **nunquam.** Translate : ' never have you desired, I will not say peace, but even war '.

l. 7. **nisi nefarium,** ' unless (it was) a wicked one '. Cicero means civil war.

l. 7. **nactus,** from **nanciscor.**

l. 8. **ab omni . . . spe,** ' not only in every (kind of) fortune but also in hopes '.

l. 9. **conflatam,** a metaphor from metal-working, ' fused *or* welded '.

l. 10. **perfruere** : parse carefully.

l. 11. **bacchabere** : **bacchor** literally means, ' celebrate the rites of Bacchus ', Greek god of wine. From the nature of the worship, the verb came to mean ' revel '. Cf. the English ' bacchanalia '.

l. 13. **ad huius vitae studium . . . otiosorum.** In this sentence the subject of **meditati sunt,** is **illi labores tui qui feruntur,** and the infinitives **iacere,** and **vigilare** are in apposition with **labores.**

Note that **meditati sunt** is to be translated as passive, ' were practised ', although **meditor** is a deponent verb.

l. 13. **illi qui feruntur labores tui,** ' those exertions of yours which are talked about ' =' those famous exercises of yours '.

l. 14. **ad obsidendum stuprum,** ' to watch for (opportunities of) vice '.

l. 17. **habes, ubi ostentes,** ' you have a chance to show '.
ostentes, final or purpose subjunctive.

l. 19. **quibus** = **et eis,** ' and by them ', = ' and by such hard-ships '.

l. 20. **senties,** ' you will find '.

l. 20. **te a consulatu reppuli,** i.e. at the consular elections for 62 B.C., held in 63 B.C. On the day before they should have been held, Cicero exposed the designs of Catiline in the senate, and took such strong precautions against violence at the actual election a few days later that Catiline was again defeated.

l. 21. **exsul,** ' as an exile ' : **consul,** ' as a consul '.

l. 22. **id quod . . . susceptum,** ' that which had been crimin-ally undertaken by you ' = ' your criminal undertaking ', subject of **nominaretur.**

l. 24. **bellum,** a name which might have been used of an attack by a consul with full powers.

CHAPTER XI

Sections 27-29

Line 2. **patriae,** ' on the part of my country ', subjective genitive, i.e. the relation between the genitive and the noun on which it depends, is the same as that between subject and verb.

l. 2. **detester ac deprecer,** ' that I may avert by entreaty and prayer '.

l. 5. **multo carior.** Note **multo,** ablative of the measure of difference and **vita mea,** ablative of comparison.

l. 6. **loquatur,** present subjunctive in the protasis of an *ideal* conditional clause.   Cf. the note on Chap. VIII, l. 1.   There is no regular apodosis owing to the length of the following clauses.

l. 7. **Tulli,** vocative of **Tullius,** Cicero's nomen. A Roman usually had three names, the **praenomen** (=our Christian name, i.e. the individual name), a **nomen** indicating his gens (or clan), and a **cognomen** indicating the branch of the clan. E.g. Marcus Tullius Cicero, Gaius Julius Caesar.

l. 7. **Tune=tu+ne** interrogative enclitic.

l. 10. **evocatorem servorum,** Sallust, however, who wrote a monograph on the Catilinarian Conspiracy, says that Catiline refused to employ slaves, although large numbers had rushed to join his camp.

l. 11. **exire . . . ut . . . videatur,** ' (so) to depart as to appear '.

l. 13. **duci . . . rapi . . . mactari imperabis,** the accusative and infinitive is sometimes used with **impero** (instead of **ut** and subj.), but *only* when the infinitive is passive.

l. 14. **summo supplicio,** ' with the direst penalties '.

l. 15. **tandem,** ' pray '. See the note on Chap. I, l. 1.

l. 16. **persaepe,** a rhetorical exaggeration. Cicero gives only one example of a **privatus** putting a citizen to death, viz. that of P. Scipio Nasica killing Tiberius Gracchus, mentioned in Chap. I, l. 20. See the note.

l. 17. **an leges.** A series of laws from the first year of the Republic (509 B.C) until a few years before Cicero's birth in 106 B.C., had given every Roman citizen the right of appeal to his fellow-citizens against a sentence of death or flogging on the part of a magistrate.

In any case, even if such a sentence was passed by the people who alone had the right to exercise such power, the accused could always anticipate or avoid it by going into exile.

l. 18. **at numquam . . . tenuerunt.** Cicero's argument that those who act against the state, thereby forfeit their rights as citizens, has no legal validity.

Cicero no doubt felt that the senate's emergency decree [1] which gave unrestricted power to the consuls, therefore suspended the working of the constitution, and that men whose actions branded them as enemies of their country, were

[1] For which, see note on Chap. I, l. 18.

automatically outlawed and unable to appeal to the laws of the state for protection.

The weak point in Cicero's position arises from the fact that this emergency decree came from the senate, not from the people, and therefore the latter were in a position to refuse to acknowledge its legality.

l. 20. **invidiam posteritatis,** note the subjective genitive, ' hatred felt by posterity '.   If the genitive were *objective*, the phrase would mean, ' hatred felt *for* posterity '.

l. 22. **hominem per te cognitum,** ' a man known by yourself ' =' a self-made man '.

l. 22. **nulla . . . maiorum,** ' without any recommendation of ancestors ' =' without the recommendation of ancestry '.

Cicero was a **novus homo,** i.e. he did not belong to a family which had previously held public office in Rome.   He was very proud of the fact that he had risen to the highest magistracy in Rome by his own exertions, and, indeed, this was no mean achievement in the closing years of the Republic, when a comparatively few ruling families were anxious to keep all the posts for themselves to the rigid exclusion of new talent, however able and efficient.   In this close oligarchy, we see one of the reasons why the Roman Republic failed to solve the numerous problems which arose, and so collapsed.

l. 23. **tam mature.**   A law of 180 B.C.[1] fixed the lowest age at which a citizen could hold the various magistracies.   A generation before this speech of Cicero, Sulla revised these ages and outlined the order in which various political offices could be held.   So we get first, the quaestorship, minimum age 30, next, the praetorship (38), and, finally, the consulship, minimum age 43.

In another speech [2] Cicero proudly states that he was the only one of the **novi homines** who, so far as could be remembered, attained the consulship at the minimum age.

l. 26. **quis,** ' any ', as often after **si, nisi, num, ne.**

l. 27. **severitatis . . . invidia,** ' the unpopularity attaching

---

[1] Lex Villia Annalis.   [2] *De Lege Agr.*, II, 2.

to severity and firmness '. Note the *objective* genitives **severitatis** and **fortitudinis** and the way in which they are translated.

l. 28. **inertiae ac nequitiae,** supply **invidia,** ' that attaching to inactivity . . .'.

CHAPTER XII

Sections 29–30

Line 1. **His sanctissimis . . . vocibus,** ' to these most solemn words '.

l. 3. **si . . . iudicarem, . . . non dedissem.** Note that the protasis of this conditional clause is *unreal* in *present* time (imperfect subjunctive), while the apodosis is *unreal* in *past* time (pluperfect subjunctive).

l. 3. **optimum factu,** ' best in the doing ' =' the best thing to do ', **factu,** ablative of the supine (an ablative of respect).

l. 4. **Catilinam . . . multari,** in apposition with **hoc,** l. 3.

l. 5. **unius,** ' of a single '.

l. 6. **summi viri, clarissimi cives.** The former are the magistrates mentioned in Chap. II, l. 1–6, the latter the **privati** of Chap. I, l. 20. For the incidents referred to see the notes on these chapters.

This sentence seems to be an answer to the question of Chap. XI, l. 15. **Quid tandem te impedit ? Mosne maiorum ?**

Cicero has no answer to the second question **An leges,** because there was in existence no law to which he could appeal. In fact, as we pointed out in the note on that passage, the laws were directly against him.

l. 9. **verendum mihi non erat,** ' it was not to-be-feared by me ', =' I had not to fear '.

l. 10. **ne,** ' that ' or ' lest '.

l. 10. **quid . . . invidiae,** ' anything of unpopularity ', =' any unpopularity '. **invidiae,** partitive gen.

l. 10. **hoc . . . interfecto,** ablative absolute, best translated by a causal clause.

l. 12. **hoc animo,** ablative of quality or description. This ablative always consists of a noun and adjective.

l. 12. **ut . . . putarem : partam** is the perf. part. pass. of **pario,** and **gloriam, non invidiam** is the complement to **invidiam . . . partam (esse).**

l. 14. **qui . . . videant : qui** =tales **ut ei,** ' of such a kind that they ' : hence the subjunctive is consecutive.

l. 16. **qui . . . aluerunt . . . corroboraverunt.** Note that **qui** is here followed by the indicative. Therefore this clause is not parallel with the previous **qui** consecutive clauses. **Qui** = ' and they '.

l. 16. **spem,** ' hopes '.

l. 16. **mollibus sententiis,** ' by lenient speeches '—a reference to the meeting of the senate which preceded the consular elections. See the note on Chap. X, l. 20 and the Introduction.

l. 19. **si . . . animadvertissem . . . dicerent ;** note the protasis, *unreal* in *past* time, and the apodosis, *unreal* in *present* time : ' if I had punished, . . . they would now be saying '.

l. 20. **factum esse,** *lit.,* ' that it was done ', =' that I had acted '.

l. 20. **regie,** ' despotically '. Cicero is anticipating an accusation which was later often made against him by his political enemies, viz., that he had abused his consular power.

l. 24. **hoc . . . interfecto :** abl. absol., best translated by a conditional ' if ' clause.

l. 26. **reprimi, non . . . comprimi posse.** For the asyndeton (absence of a conjunction), see the note on Chap. I, l. 20.

l. 28. **naufragos,** ' castaways ', *or* ' ship-wrecked crew '.

CHAPTER XIII

Sections 31-33

Line 1. **iam diu . . . versamur.** For the tense (present = English perfect), see the note on Chap. II, l. 10.

l. 1. **in his periculis coniurationis,** ' in these dangers of a conspiracy ' =' in this dangerous conspiracy '.

l. 2. **nescio quo pacto,** *lit.,* ' I know not in what way ' = ' somehow or other '. This phrase is used parenthetically, i.e. without any grammatical influence on the rest of the sentence. Cf. the use of the French, *je ne sais quoi.*

l. 4. **maturitas,** ' full force '.

l. 5. **ex tanto latrocinio,** abstract for concrete, ' from this great force of brigands '.

l. 6. **cura et metu,** ablatives of separation with **relevati.**

l. 8. **ut,** ' as '.

l. 9. **aestu febrique,** hendiadys,[1] ' in feverish heat '.

l. 10. **iactantur = se iactant,** ' toss themselves " = ' toss '. The passive is often used in Latin with a reflexive or middle meaning.

l. 12. **relevatus istius poena,** ' (if it is) relieved by the punishment of this fellow '.

l. 13. **reliquis vivis,** ' the rest (being) alive ' = ' as long as the rest remain alive '.

l. 14. **secedant,** jussive subjunctive, ' let the wicked depart ' ; similarly **secernant, congregentur,** etc.

l. 15. **quod,** ' as '.

l. 17. **domi suae,** locative case, ' in his own home '.

l. 17. **praetoris urbani,** ' of the city praetor '. The **praetor urbanus** was the magistrate who administered justice between Roman citizens.

l. 20. **quid de re publica sentiat,** ' what he feels about the state ' = ' his political sentiments '. Take this as the subject of **sit inscriptum.**

l. 24. **Catilinae profectione,** ' on Catiline's departure '.

l. 25. **omnia,** ' the whole conspiracy '.

l. 27. **cum . . . salute, cum tua peste,** *lit.,* ' with the complete salvation ' . . . Translate ' to the complete salvation, . . ., to you own ruin and destruction . . .'.

[1] *lit.,* ' one thing by means of two ' : i.e. two co-ordinate words are used instead of an expression in which one qualifies the other.

l. 31. **Tu, Iuppiter.** Cicero now turns to the statue of Jupiter Stator in whose temple the senate is met.

l. 31. **qui . . . constitutus,** ' who was established by Romulus under the same auspices as this city '. Cicero is using rhetorical exaggeration because while Romulus vowed to erect, the temple, it was not built until nearly five hundred years later, 294 B.C.

l. 32. **Statorem,** ' the Stablisher ' or ' Protector '. This meaning is slightly different from that in which, according to Livy's story, Bk. I, 12, Romulus hailed the god as the ' Stayer of Flight '.

l. 37. **inter se,** ' with one another '.

l. 38. **aeternis,** ' never-ending ' or ' unending '.

l. 38. **vivos mortuosque,** ' in life and in death '.

SECOND SPEECH

CHAPTER I

Sections 1-2

Line 1. **Quirites,** a term which, once applied to the oldest inhabitants of Rome, came to be used of the Roman citizens in their civil capacity.

Cicero is addressing his second speech against Catiline to the people,—a fact which partly accounts for the accumulation of synonyms and the rather forced style of the first chapter.

l. 2. **pestem,** object of **molientem.**

l. 4. **eiecimus, . . . emisimus . . . ;** translate by 1st pers. sing.

l. 4. **emisimus,** ' I have allowed to go '.

l. 4. **vel . . . vel . . . vel. Vel,** from **volo** (*lit.,* ' you may choose') gives a choice and suggests here that you may take which verb you like. **Aut,** on the other hand, implies a strong contrast : e.g. **vita aut mors,** ' life or death '.

l. 5. **verbis prosecuti sumus,** ' I escorted with words ' = ' I wished him " bon voyage " '.

l. 7. **moenibus ipsis,** ' against the very walls ', dative.

l. 11. **versabitur,** ' will remain '.

l. 13. **loco ille motus est,** ' he is driven from his ground '— an expression taken from the language of prize-fighting.

l. 14. **cum,** ' in that '. When the actions of the two clauses are coincident, **cum** almost = **quod,** ' in that '. Cf. Cat. I, Chap. VIII, l. 36, **cum tacent, clamant.**

l. 14. **nullo impediente,** abl. absol. **Nullo,** ablative of **nemo.**

l. 14. **iustum,** ' regular '.

l. 17. **quod vero,** ' as to the fact that '.

l. 18. **cruentum,** predicative, ' blood-stained '.

l. 19. **ei . . . de manibus,** ' from his hands ' : **ei,** dative of the

71

person interested, conveniently translated by English possessive adjective ' his '.

l. 21. **tandem,** ' pray '.

l. 24. **profecto,** an adverb, ' certainly ', ' assuredly ',
strengthening the preceding **et,** which, here, adds a climax.

l. 25. **quae quidem.** You will often have noticed that
Roman writers frequently begin fresh sentences with relative
pronouns, and that it is better to translate them by ' this ',
' he ', ' she ', etc., in English. Here **quae** strengthened by
quidem = sed ea, ' but she '.

l. 26. **quod . . . evomuerit . . . proiecerit,** the subjunctives
are due to the causal clause being sub-oblique, i.e. being
virtually in oratio obliqua, indirect speech, ' because (as she
thinks) . . .'.

CHAPTER II

Sections 3-4

Line 1. **talis . . . quales,** ' of such a character . . . as '.
Note **qualis,** used as the correlative of **talis.**

l. 1. **oportebat,** for the construction (acc. and infin.), cf.
Chap. I of the First Speech, l. 18.

l. 2. **in hoc ipso,** ' in this very matter '.

l. 3. **quod . . . comprehenderim . . . emiserim,** ' because (as
he says) . . .'. See the note on l. 26 above.

l. 8. **mos maiorum,,** ' tradition ', *lit.,* ' the custom of our
ancestors '. **res publica,** ' (the interests of) the state '.

This sentence would run better in English, if it were turned
from the active into the passive, ' and this was demanded of
me by . . .'.

l. 10. **qui . . . non crederent,** consecutive subjunctive, for
qui = tales ut ei, ' of such a kind that they '.

l. 11. **defenderent,** ' tried to justify it '.

ll. 11-14. **ac si . . . iudicarem, . . . sustulissem ;** note the
protasis (imperf. subj.), unreal in *present* time, ' if I thought '
(*but I do not*), . . . the apodosis, unreal in *past* time, ' I would
have destroyed ' (*but I did not*).

l. 11. **illo sublato,** 'he (having been) removed'='by his removal'.

l. 13. **invidiae meae . . . periculo,** 'at the risk of my gaining unpopularity'.

l. 14. **ne vobis . . . probata,** *lit.*, 'the fact even then proved not even to you all'='at a time when you were not all convinced of the fact'.

l. 14. **cum viderem . . . fore ut . . . non possem,** 'when I saw . . . it would be that . . . I could not'='when I saw . . . that I would not be able'. **Fore ut,** as a periphrasis for the future infinitives, is used chiefly with verbs that do not form the future participle.

l. 17. **rem huc deduxi,** 'I brought the matter to this point'.

ll. 19-21. **quem quidem . . . intellegatis.** Note: (i) **quem quidem hostem,** see the note on Chap. I, l. 25 above. (ii) **putem,** subjunctive in indirect question, dependent on **intellegatis.** (iii) **licet intellegatis,** 'it is allowed (that) you perceive'='you may perceive'.

l. 21. **illud . . . quod,** 'that'.

l. 21. **moleste fero,** 'I bear ill'='I am annoyed'.

l. 22. **parum comitatus,** 'little accompanied'='with so few followers'. Note **comitatus,** the perf. part. of a deponent verb, used in a *passive* sense.

l. 23. **Tongilium, . . . Publicium . . . Minucium,** probably names of men who were well known only for their crimes or vices.

l. 23. **mihi,** a good example of what is known as the *ethic* dative, which is included in the same class as the dative of the *person interested.* Translate here by 'I find'.

l. 24. **in praetexta.** A Roman boy wore the **toga praetexta** (embroidered with a purple stripe) until he was about seventeen, when he put on the **toga virilis,** a plain white woollen garment, the dress of all Roman citizens. Thus **in praetexta** means 'in boyhood'.

l. 26. **nullum . . . motum,** 'no revolutionary uprising'.

CHAPTER III

Sections 5, 6

Line 1. **Gallicanis legionibus**, ' Gallic legions ', i.e. legions stationed in Gallia Cisalpina, ' Gaul this side of the Alps ' [1] which roughly corresponds to the whole of the Lombardy Plain and Italy north of the Apennines.

l. 2. **in agro Piceno et Gallico.** Picenum was a strip of land in Central Italy along the Adriatic, while the ager Gallicus seems to be the coast land of the district known as Umbria which lay to the north and west of Picenum.

l. 4. **collectum**, in agreement with **illum exercitum**, l. 1.

l. 5. **ex agresti luxuria**, ' from boorish profligacy ' = ' from profligate boors '. Note the use of the abstract noun for the concrete.

l. 6. **vadimonia deserere**, ' to desert their bail ', i.e. ' to fail to appear '.

l. 7. **quibus . . . concident** = qui (' and they ') concident, si eis non modo . . . ostendero.

l. 8. **edictum praetoris.** On taking office, the praetors published an edict which contained the rules of law by which they intended to act during their year of office. It was composed of the legal decisions of previous holders of this important magistracy.

l. 11. **unguentis.** The use of perfumes by men was considered effeminate among the Romans as it is in most countries today.

l. 12. **purpura**, ablative. Among Roman fops, it was considered fashionable to wear costly purple stuff on the edge of the **tunica**, a shirt-like garment worn underneath the **toga**.

l. 12. **mallem . . . eduxisset**, ' I would prefer that he had taken them '.

[1] From Rome.

Mallem is here used for the more usual **utinam** + the pluperfect subjunctive,[1] to express a wish for the past, now incapable of fulfilment.

l. 13. **mementote,** 2nd pl. imperative of **memini.**

l. 13. **non tam exercitum . . . pertimescendos,** ' (that it is) not so much that army (that) is to be feared by us (=we have to fear) as those who . . .'.

l. 15. **hoc . . . magis,** ' by this the more ' = ' the more so '. Hoc, ablative of the measure of difference, found with comparatives.

l. 16. **quid cogitent,** indirect question, dependent on **me scire.**

l. 17. **sit, . . . habeat . . . depoposcerit,** subjunctives in indirect question.

l. 17. **Apulia,** a district east of the Apennines, above the ' heel ' of Italy.

l. 18. **Etruriam ;** Etruria was the district north of the Tiber, inhabited in early times by the Etruscans, about whose origin little is known. In the first quarter of the first millenium B.C., they were a powerful nation, noted for their building, their mine-working, and extensive commercial interests. It is now known that in many ways, particularly in religious rites and methods of divination, they had considerable influence on the Romans.

l. 19. **has urbanas . . . incendiorum,** ' this city plot of murder and fire ' = ' this treacherous role of spreading fire and death throughout the city '.

l. 20. **superioris noctis,** ' of the night before last '. Actually it was three nights ago. Cicero is thinking in terms of the speech which he delivered in the senate, the day before.

l. 23. **ne,** interjection = ' truly ' *or* ' verily '.

---

[1] See Chap. II, l. 22, utinam . . . eduxisset.

CHAPTER IV

Sections 6-8

Line 1. **quod**, relative pronoun, ' what '.

l. 3. **nisi si quis est**, ' except in case there is anyone '.

l. 3. **Catilinae similes**, ' men like Catiline '.

l. 4. **cum Catilina sentire**, ' feel with Catiline ' =' have the same political opinions as Catiline '.

l. 5. **locus**, ' room '.

l. 6. **exeant; proficiscantur; ne patiantur**, jussive subjunctives; ' let them leave . . .'.

l. 7. **desiderio sui**, ' in longing for them '. Note **sui**, objective genitive, referring to the subject of **patiantur**.

l. 8. **Aurelia via**, ablative case. This road ran along the west coast of Italy from Rome to Pisa. This was not the direct route to Manlius' camp, but Catiline wished to give the impression that he was on his way to Marseilles, to go into exile.

l. 9. **O fortunatam rem publicam**, accusative of exclamation.

l. 11. **mehercule**. See the note on Chap. VII of Book I, l. 13.

l. 11. **uno Catilina exhausto**, abl. absol. Translate by an ' if ' clause. **exhausto** (from **exhaurio**, *lit.*, ' drain out '), continues the metaphor of **sentina**, *lit.*, ' bilge-water '.

l. 13. **Quid mali aut sceleris**, ' what evil or crime '. Note the partitive genitive.

l. 14. **conceperit**, consecutive subjunctive, for **quod** =**tale ut id**, ' of such a kind that it '.

l. 14. **tota Italia**, ablative of place where, ' throughout the whole of Italy '. Note that with **totus, medius**, no preposition is used.

l. 14. **quis . . . veneficus**, etc., ' what poisoner'.

l. 19. **qui . . . fateatur**, ' as to admit '. **fateatur**, consecutive subjunctive.

l. 19. **se . . . non familiarissime vixisse**, ' that he has not been on the most intimate terms '.

l. 22. **quae ... quanta.** **tanta ... quanta,** ' so great ... as ' : **iuventutis,** objective genitive, dependent on **illecebra** ; **tanta,** take as the complement after **fuit.**

l. 24. **amori,** ' passion ', dative depending on **serviebat.**

l. 25. **aliis . . . aliis,** ' to some . . . to others ', dependent on **pollicebatur,** l. 27.

l. 25. ,**fructum,** ' enjoyment '.

l. 26. **impellendo,** ' by urging '.

l. 27. **quam,** ' how '.

l. 30. **Romae,** locative, ' in Rome '.

CHAPTER V ,

Sections 9-11

Line 1. **in dissimili ratione,** ' in a very different sphere '.

l. 2. **in ludo gladiatorio.** When displays of gladiators became popular in Italy at the great public games, training schools were established, especially in Capua in Central Italy. Cicero mentions that there were 5,000 gladiators in this town. They were recruited from prisoners of war, condemned criminals or slaves. In addition to their appearance in public shows, they were maintained as private armies by individuals in Cicero's time.

l. 4. **in scaena.** Actors on the Roman stage were generally slaves or freedmen, for acting was not considered the profession of a freeman.

l. 6. **stuprorum . . . perferendis,** ' (when) by the practice of his vices and crimes (he had grown) hardened (**adsuefactus**) to the endurance of cold, hunger, thirst and lack of sleep (**vigilia**) '.

l. 9. **cum,** ' although '.

l. 9. **industriae subsidia atque instrumenta virtutis,** ' the means of industry and the resources of virtue '. By the former Cicero means physical power, by the latter moral power.

l. 13. **o nos beatos,** etc., accusatives of exclamation.

l. 14. **laudem,** ' achievement '.

l. 14. **mediocres,** ' ordinary ', complement after **sunt.** Similarly, **humanae et tolerandae.**

l. 16. **audaciae,** ' acts of daring '. Latin often uses the plural of abstract nouns in a concrete meaning : cf. **amicitiae** = ' friends '.

l. 18. **res,** ' money ' ; **fides,** ' credit ' : **nuper,** especially since the consular elections when Catiline's failure to be elected meant the collapse of their revolutionary schemes.

l. 19. **eadem illa,** in agreement with **libido.**

l. 19. **quae erat in abundantia,** ' which was (to them) in their prosperity ', =' which they had when they were well-off '.

l. 21. **solum,** adv., ' only '.

l. 22. **essent . . . ferendi,** *lit.,* ' they would be to-be-despaired of, but yet they would be to-be-endured ' =' we might despair of them, but still, we should have to put up with them '.

l. 23. **inertes homines,** ' the idle '.

l. 24. **dormientes,** ' the sleeping ' ; **vigilantibus,** ' the watchful '.

l. 25. **mihi,** ethic dative, =' I find '. See the note on Chap. II, l. 23.

l. 26. **complexi,** ' holding in their arms '.

l. 27. **obliti,** perf. part. pass. from **oblino,** ' I smear '.

l. 28. **eructant . . . incendia,** *lit.,* ' belch out in their talk the murder of loyal citizens, etc.' =' talk in drunken hiccups of the murder . . .'.

l. 30. **quibus** =et eis, dative after **impendere.**

l. 33. **quos** =et eos, object of **sanare** and **sustulerit.**

l. 34. **non breve . . . rei publicae.** Note : (i) **nescio quod,** *lit.,* ' I know not what ' =' some ', to be taken with **breve tempus,** object (as is **multa saecula**) of **propagarit.** (ii) **propagarit** =propagaverit, fut. perfect, =' it will be found to have prolonged '. (iii) **rei publicae,** dative.

l. 36. **quam pertimescamus,** consecutive subjunctive, ' for us to fear '. Similarly **qui . . . possit.**

l. 38. **unius,** i.e. of Pompey the Great, who had defeated the powerful Mithridates in Asia Minor on land (**terrā**), and cleared the pirates from the Eastern Mediterranean (**mari**).

l. 41. **nobis certandum est,** ' there is to be a striving by us ' =' we have to strive '. Note once again the gerundive in the nominative expressing ' ought ', ' must ', ' should '.

l. 43. **quae . . . poterunt,** object of **sanabo,** l. 44.

l. 44. **quacumque ratione,** supply **potero,** ' by whatever means I can '.

l. 47. **in eadem mente,** ' in the same (frame of) mind '.

Note that with **in urbe,** the verb **permanent** is used in a literal meaning, but with **in mente** in a metaphorical one. This figure of speech is known as syllepsis, and is used in English chiefly in burlesque : cf. Dickens', ' Mr. Weller then took his hat and his leave '.

CHAPTER VI
Sections 12-14

Line 1. **sunt qui dicant,** ' there are such as say ' =' some say '.

l. 2. **si . . . possem, . . . eicerem.** Note the mood and tense of this conditional clause, unreal in present time.

l. 3. **verbo,** ' with a single (*or* mere) word '.

l. 4. **homo . . . non potuit,** sarcastic ; ' evidently (**videlicet**) the nervous or even docile fellow . . .'.

l. 5. **simul atque,** ' as soon as '.

l. 6. **hesterno die.** Here Cicero begins to answer the objection given at the beginning of the chapter, **sunt qui dicant,** etc.

l. 9. **quo,** relative adverb, ' whither ' =' and hither ' =' and here '.

l. 10. **appellavit,** ' spoke to him '.

l. 11. **ita,** need not be translated ; **ut,** ' as '.

l. 12. **importunissimum,** ' most cruel '.

l. 12. **quin,** ' nay '.

l. 16. **in nocturno . . . necne** ; supply ' whether ' before this indirect question : **necne,** ' or not '.

l. 18. **ille . . . audacissimus,** ' that insolent fellow '.

l. 18. **conscientia,** abl., ' consciousness (of his guilt) .

l. 20. **quem ad modum . . . descripta,** ' how the plan of the whole campaign had been developed by him '. This indirect question and the preceding ones, **quid . . . constituisset,** are dependent on **edocui,** l. 21.

l. 22. **cum teneretur,** ' when he was caught '.

l. 23. **quo . . . pararet,** ' whither (=where) he had long been preparing to go '. For the Latin imperfect with **iam pridem** =English pluperfect, cf. the note on the First Speech, Chap. II, l. 10.

l. 23. **cum arma . . . .** cum =' when ', and **arma, secures, fasces, tubas, signa militaria, aquilam illam argenteam** are all subjects of **esse praemissam,** in the accusative and infinitive construction, object of **scirem.**

secures, fasces. Consuls and higher magistrates in Rome were attended by a personal bodyguard of men, called lictors, who carried on their left shoulders an axe bound in a bundle of rods. The axe and the rods were believed to symbolise the power to flog and to execute. As only magistrates entitled to the fasces had the power (**imperium**) to command an army of Roman citizens, Catiline, in employing a bodyguard with the fasces, was usurping a power which he had failed to obtain at the consular elections.

l. 27. **eiciebam,** ' I tried to expel '. Note the force of the imperfect.

l. 27. **quem,** ' (one) whom '.

l. 28. **etenim, credo, . . .** Cicero is using rather a heavy sarcasm.

l. 29. **in agro Faesulano,** ' in the district of Faesulae ', i.e. about 5 miles from the modern Florence. Manlius' camp dominated a pass on the western Apennines which led northwards into the Lombardy plain, southwards into Etruria.

l. 32. **se . . . conferet,** ' will betake himself '.

CHAPTER VII

Sections 14-16

Line 1. **O condicionem miseram,** 'what a poor method', acc. of exclamation.

l. 3. **nunc si . . .** The protasis ('if' clause) extends down to **converterit,** l. 7. Note that Latin uses future perfect, where we have the present, in the protasis of 'open' conditional clauses, with a future in the apodosis.

l. 4. **debilitatus,** 'crippled'.

l. 7. **non ille . . . dicetur,** *lit.,* 'he will be said not to have been spoiled by me by the weapons of courage, not to have been dazed . . ., but to have been expelled . . .'. We prefer to say: 'it will be said, not that he was spoiled . . ., but that he was expelled . . .'.

l. 10. **indemnatus,** 'unsentenced'.

l. 11. **vi et minis,** 'by violence and threats' = 'by violent threats'. Note the hendiadys,[1] i.e. Latin uses two nouns to express one idea, rendered in English by a combination of adjective and noun.

l. 11. **erunt qui . . . velint,** 'there will be (some) such as wish' = 'some will wish'.

l. 14. **est mihi tanti . . . subire,** 'it is worth so much to me' = 'it is worth my while to undergo'.

l. 15. **dum modo,** 'provided only'.

l. 17. **dicatur,** jussive -subj., 'let him be said'. For the personal construction in Latin, cf. the note on l. 7 above.

l. 18. **non est iturus,** 'he is not intending to go'.

l. 20. **invidiae . . . causa.** Note: (i) **causa,** 'for the sake of', +gen., following its case. (ii) the gerundive construction, which in the genitive is an alternative for the gerund +a direct object, e.g. **invidiam relevandi.**

l. 22. **illud,** 'the following', *or* 'this', explained by the **ne** clause.

[1] *Lit.,* 'one through two'.

l. 23. **aliquando,** ' one day '.

l. 24. **emiserim,** ' I let him go '.

l. 25. **cum,** ' since '.

l. 25. **qui . . . dicant,** ' to say '. Note the consecutive subjunctive.

l. 26. **idem, si interfectus esset, quid dicerent?** Note the difference in *tense* in this conditional clause. ' If he had been put to death, what would the same men be saying *now*? '

l. 28. **non tam . . . quam,** ' not so much . . . as '.

l. 29. **qui . . . malit,** ' as to prefer '. Cf. l. 25 above.

l. 30. **quam,** ' rather than '. Cicero means that if they really felt sorry for Catiline, they would prefer him to go to Marseilles to safety, rather than to the camp of Manlius and to certain destruction.

l. 32. **latrocinantem,** ' in his bandit war '.

l. 33. **cum,** ' since '.

l. 35. **nisi quod,** ' except that '.

l. 35. **vivis nobis,** abl. absol., ' us alive ' = ' whilst we still remain alive '.

l. 35. **optemus,** jussive subjunctive, which, when in the 1st person, is usually known as hortative.

l. 36. **queramur.** Cicero means that as yet they have not any reason to complain.

CHAPTER VIII

Sections 17-18

line 3. **quod,** ' as '.

l. 3. **timeo ; de his . . .** Note the asyndeton, for which see the note on the First Speech, Chap. I, l. 20. We might supply ' while ' or ' but '.

l. 7. **sibi . . . rei publicae,** ' for themselves, . . . for the state ' = ' for their own interests, . . . for the interest of the state '. Cicero suggests that he wishes to bring the followers of Catiline to their senses, suffering as they are from a kind of moral disorder.

l. 9. **ex quibus generibus.** In dividing the conspirators into six types and giving a brilliant sketch of their general characteristics, Cicero no doubt hopes to dispel any uneasiness that may have arisen in Rome from the many exaggerated reports of the strength and extent of the conspiracy.

l. 11. **si quam potero,** *lit.,* ' if I shall be able (to apply) any '. **quam** is the fem. acc. sing. of the indefinite pronoun **quis** = ' any ' after **si, nisi, num, ne.**

l. 12. **adferam,** ' I shall apply '.

l. 13. **magno,** ' deeply '.

l. 14. **quarum,** ' for which ', objective genitive depending on **amore.**

l. 15. **dissolvi,** ' get out of debt '. The verb also contains the meaning ' be torn (from them) '. Cicero means that these men, deep in debt, yet possessing vast estates, are too fond of their property to sell them in order to pay their debts.

At this time, however, owing to the insecurity caused by the designs of Catiline, property had dropped greatly in value, so that it is unlikely that the owners could have obtained enough money from a sale to pay their debts.

l. 17. **causa,** ' case '.

l. 17. **tu,** etc. Cicero now addresses himself to a representative of this class.

l. 19. **sis,** ' (though) you are '.

l. 19. **et dubites . . . ad fidem,** ' yet you would hesitate to lose (anything) of your estates and gain as regards credit? '

Hence Cicero calls their case **impudentissima** in l. 17, because they could easily have paid their debts before the depreciation of property caused by their own conspiracy, but refused to do so.

l. 21. **in vastatione omnium,** ' in the devastation of everything ' = ' in the universal devastation '.

l. 22. **tabulas novas,** supply **exspectas. Tabulae novae,** ' new account books ' = ' cancellation of debts '—one of the aims of Catiline.

l. 24. **tabulae novae . . . auctionariae,** ' a cancellation of debts is suggested, but by selling goods by auction '.

During his consulship Cicero attempted to grapple with this problem of debt and the general collapse of credit by compelling debtors to surrender a portion of their property in part payment of their debts.

l. 26. **salvi,** ' (financially) sound *or* saved '.

l. 26. **quod,** ' this ', object of **facere** ; i.e. the surrendering of a portion of their estates. Cf. the note above, l. 24.

l. 27. **id quod,** ' what '.

l. 28. **certare . . . praediorum,** ' to struggle with the interest by means of the produce of their estates '.

As these rich men vainly attempt to pay off the interest on their debts with the produce of their estates, Cicero calls this foolish behaviour a struggle (**certare**) in which the produce is always fighting a losing battle with the interest.

l. 29. **uteremur,** *lit.*, ' we should use ' ; translate ' we should find '. Note that **utor** is followed by the ablative case.

CHAPTER IX

Sections 19-20

Line 1. **alterum,** ' second '.

l. 1. **quamquam . . .** Note the political thought here. Cicero assumes as a well-attested principle that the possession of property is the basis of all political power.

l. 3. **quieta re publica,** abl. absol., ' when the state is calm '. Similarly **perturbata (re publica),** l. 4.

l. 4. **consequi,** ' attain '.

l. 5. **quibus . . . videtur,** ' to whom this seems is to-be-taught ', i.e. ' it seems that we must teach them this '.

l. 5. **unum scilicet . . . omnibus,** ' one and the same thing, of course (**scilicet**), as all the rest '. **Reliquis omnibus** is dat. balancing **quibus.**

l. 6. **ut,** ' (namely) that they should despair, etc.'

l. 7. **primum me . . . vigilare, adesse,** etc. Notice that after the colon, l. 7, the Latin slips into indirect speech. Supply some such words as ' let them remember '.

l. 13. **praesentes,** ' present ', is emphatic. Translate ' in visible presence ' or ' with power '.

l. 14. **sint . . . adepti.** Order for translating : **quod si iam adepti sint id quod . . .** Note **quod si** introducing a conditional clause, ' ideal ' type : ' now if they should obtain '.

l. 15. **num,** ' surely . . . not ', introduces a question which *expects* the answer ' no '.

l. 16. **quae,** neuter plural, referring to the antecedents **cinere** and **sanguine.** Note that, when there are several antecedents of different genders and representing things, the relative pronoun is put in the neuter.

l. 19. **concedi sit necesse,** ' would have to be yielded '.

l. 21. **Tertium genus.** The third class consists of veteran soldiers who had fought in Sulla's victorious campaigns in the East 87-84 B.C.[1] against Mithridates, a prince who lived on the south shores of the Black Sea and at the time seemed likely to overthrow the Roman power in Asia Minor.

l. 21. **aetate adfectum,** ' burdened by age '.

l. 23. **Manlius,** formerly a centurion of Sulla who had had much military experience.

l. 23. **succedit,** ' succeeds,' ' takes the place of '.

l. 24. **quas Sulla constituit.** In the first century B.C., after Marius had turned the old Roman militia into a professional army, it became customary to give grants of land to soldiers, discharged after a campaign. In most cases during the civil wars which marked Roman history from Marius to Augustus, a period of seventy years (100–31 B.C.), land for allotment was obtained by taking it from the supporters of the losing side.

One Roman historian, Appian,[2] gives the number of soldiers settled on the land by Sulla as 120,000. In this case many

---

[1] *I.e.* over twenty years before the time of this speech.
[2] Writing at the end of the first century A.D.

were settled in Etruria (north of Rome), for its inhabitants had been most active against the Roman general.

These colonies were not successful. Many of those who received allotments soon tired of their farms after the excitements of army and camp life, and, as they tended to get into debt, they gradually formed both a serious unemployment problem and a dangerous and discontented mob, who would be anxious to retrieve their fallen fortunes by a violent or revolutionary programme.

l. 24. **quas . . . universas,** ' and these on the whole '.

l. 25. **esse,** ' consist of '.

l. 26. **sed tamen . . . coloni,** =' but still among them there are colonists '.

l. 26. **se . . . iactarunt,** ' have behaved ' : **iactarunt** =**iactaverunt.**

l. 27. **sumptuosius insolentiusque,** comparative adverbs, ' too . . .'.

l. 28. **beati,** ' wealthy '.

l. 29. **adparatis,** ' elaborate '.

l. 31. **Sulla . . . excitandus,** ' Sulla is to be aroused from the world below ' =' they would have to arouse ', etc.

l. 32. **agrestes,** ' countrymen ' with which **homines tenues atque egentes** is in apposition. Probably these are the men ejected from their farms to make room for the ' colonists '.

l. 36. **proscriptiones,** ' proscriptions ', the horrible practice, begun by Marius, of posting up a list of one's political opponents who could be murdered with impunity.

l. 39. **passurae,** future participle of **patior,** ' likely to endure '.

CHAPTER X

Sections 21–23

Line 2. **turbulentum,** ' of a heterogeneous character ', i.e. drawn from all types of country and town.

l. 2. **iam pridem premuntur.** Note the Latin present where we prefer the perfect.

l. 3. **emergunt,** ' get clear (of their debts) '.

l. 3. **inertia,** ablative of cause.

l. 3. **male gerendo negotio,** ' by doing business badly ', i.e. by failure in business '.

l. 4. **vetere,** ' long-standing '.

l. 5. **vadimoniis, iudiciis, proscriptione bonorum,** ' by (frequently) going bail, by court decisions, and by public sale of their property '.
In bankruptcy proceedings, the parties entered into a **vadimonium** to appear in court; then after the action had taken place and judgment been delivered, if the bankrupt failed to discharge his obligations within a fixed date, his goods (**bona**) were distrained, and sold publicly by auction.

l. 6. **permulti,** ' in very large numbers ', *lit.,* ' very many '.

l. 8. **infitiatores lentos,** *lit.,* ' tardy refusers ' : here perhaps best translated by ' indolent shirkers '. By a ' tardy refuser ', Cicero refers to that type of man who has always an excuse to avoid payment of debt or obligation.

l. 10. **corruant,** ' would collapse '.

l. 11. **illud,** omit in translation. The pronoun merely anticipates or points to the following indirect question—**quam ob rem.**

l. 13. **turpiter,** ' disgracefully ', i.e. in fighting against their own country.

l. 18. **pereant,** jussive subjunctive, ' let them perish '.

l. 18. **ita,** merely = **tam** here.

l. 19. **carcer.** At this time there was only one prison in Rome. This contained one chamber called the Tullianum where sentences of death were executed, and another for temporary detention until sentence had been delivered. It is important to remember that the Romans did not use imprisonment as a method of punishment.

l. 19. **capere,** ' hold '.

l. 20. **numero,** ablative of respect : so also **genere ipso atque vita.**

l. 21. **proprium Catilinae,** ' Catiline's own (bodyguard) '.

l. 21. **de eius dilectu . . . ac sinu,** *lit.,* ' of his selection, yes indeed of his embrace and bosom ' =' his selected and most intimate friends '.

l. 23. **aut imberbes aut bene barbatos,** ' either smooth-chinned (*lit.,* beardless) or with a full beard '. The former adjective denotes effeminacy and the latter foppishness. It is believed that it was customary for a Roman to shave his beard for the first time on his twenty-first birthday and to let it grow only in time of mourning. There is another view, however, that it was only about the age of forty that Romans shaved completely.

l. 24. **manicatis et talaribus tunicis.** It was considered unseemly among the Romans at this time to wear the tunic with long sleeves, or reaching down to the ankles.

l. 24. **velis amictos.** Similarly it was unseemly to wear too wide a toga.

l. 26. **in antelucanis cenis,** ' in banquets lasting till dawn '.

l. 29. **neque,** ' not (only) '.

l. 32. **scitote,** an old form of the imperative mood, 2nd person plural.

l. 33. **quid sibi isti volunt?** Note **volo,** with acc. of thing and dat. of person, in the meaning, ' what are they driving at ? ', ' what is their object ? '.

l. 34. **num,** ' surely . . . not '.

l. 34. **sunt . . . ducturi,** ' intend to take '.

l. 36. **his . . . noctibus.** The date of Cicero's speech was Nov. 8th, but in his day,[1] the Roman calendar was about two months behind the real season of the year.

l. 38. **idcirco . . . quod,** ' for the reason that '.

l. 39. **O bellum . . . pertimescendum,** accusative of exclamation.

l. 40. **cum,** ' since '. Note that in this meaning **cum** is followed by the subjunctive mood.

---

[1] *I.e.* before the correction made by Julius Caesar.

l. 41. **cohortem praetoriam,** ' bodyguard '. The bodyguard of a Roman general consisted originally of his closest friends, but about this time it was made up usually of picked professional soldiers.

CHAPTER XI

Sections 24–25

Line 2. **praesidia,** ' defences '.

l. 3. **gladiatori . . . saucio,** i.e. Catiline. Cicero describes him as wounded because he had been driven out of his secret conspiracy into the open.

l. 5. **eiectam,** ' stranded '.

l. 6. **florem, . . . robur,** ' the flower . . . and pride '.
robur, *lit.,* ' hard wood ', is often used metaphorically for ' the best part ', ' the kernel ', ' the pride ' of an army. Note that it is here used as a synonym for **flos.**

l. 7. **municipiorum.** The term **municipium** embraced all the Italian towns which had by this time been granted full Roman citizenship. They retained their own government for purely local affairs. On the other hand, a **colonia** was essentially of Roman foundation.

l. 7. **respondebunt,** ' will give an answer to ' = ' will be a match for '.

l. 8. **tumulis silvestribus,** ' the wooded mounds '.
Cicero sarcastically calls Catiline's military position ' mere wooded mounds ' and contrasts them with the fortified towns and colonies of Italy.

l. 9. **copias,** ' resources '.

l. 9. **ornamenta,** ' equipment '.

l. 9. **praesidia,** ' garrison forces '.

l. 11. **quibus nos suppeditamur, eget ille,** ' with which we are supplied, (but which), he lacks'. Note the asyndeton, or absence of a conjunction in Latin. This is common where a contrast is required.

Note also the arrangement of the words, i.e. pronoun, verb, verb, pronoun, i.e., a, b, b, a. This is known as chiasmus.[1]

l. 12. **senatu . . . exteris nationibus.** All these ablatives are in apposition with **his rebus,** l. 11.

l. 14. **causas ipsas . . . contendere.** ' to compare the very causes '. Note this meaning of **contendere.**

l. 15. **inter se,** ' with one another '.

l. 16. **illi,** ' the enemy ', i.e. the Catilinarians. **Ille** is often used of the other side or party.

l. 16. **iaceant,** ' are inferior '.

l. 17. **ex hac parte . . . illinc,** ' on this side . . . on that '. **Illinc,** *lit.*, ' from that side '.

l. 18. **fides,** ' loyalty '.

l. 19. **pietas,** ' duty '.

l. 19. **constantia,** ' steadfastness '.

l. 21. **aequitas,** ' justice '. **Temperantia . . . prudentia.** These with **aequitas** are the four cardinal virtues of the Socratic and Stoic schools of philosophy. The latter in particular made a strong appeal to serious-minded Romans, as it emphasised the need for the very qualities which they thought had made their country great.

l. 25. **bona ratio,** ' a good (political) theory '.

l. 26. **cum omnium . . . desperatione,** ' with universal despair '.

l. 27. **in eius modi certamine ac proelio,** ' in a contest and struggle of this kind ' = ' in such a struggle . . .'.

l. 28. **si . . . deficiant , . . . cogant,** a good example of a conditional clause of the *ideal* type, i.e. one in which the condition is put forth as possible but not likely to occur in future time. ' Should the exertions of men fail, surely (**nonne,** l. 28) the gods would compel . . .'.

l. 30. **tot et tanta vitia,** ' so many and so great vices ' is the usual Latin for ' so many terrible vices '.

[1] From the shape of the Greek letter χ (chi).

CHAPTER XII

Sections 26–27

Line 1. **quem ad modum,** ' as '.

l. 3–5. **mihi . . . consultum atque provisum est,** *lit.,* ' by me (dat. of the person interested) there has been care taken and provision made '. Note the two verbs in the impersonal passive, and compare **pugnatur,** ' there is fighting ', ' men fight ', ' a fight is going on '.

Translate, ' I have taken care and made provision '.

l. 3. **sine vestro motu,** *lit.,* ' without your disturbance ' = ' without any disturbance to you '. Note that the possessive adjective **vester** is used instead of the objective genitive.

l. 4. **satis . . . praesidii,** ' sufficient protection '; **praesidii,** partitive genitive.

l. 5. **coloni, municipes.** The difference between a **colonia** and a **municipium** has been already explained in the note on Chap. XI, l. 7. At this time the natives of both types of towns were Roman citizens, but the former, being originally a Roman foundation and not an Italian town incorporated in the Roman state perhaps as a result of conquest, had the greater prestige.

l. 7. **Gladiatores, quam . . . manum.** Note that **quam,** the antecedent of which is **gladiatores,** is attracted into the gender and number of the complement **manum.**

l. 9. **animo meliore,** abl. of description, ' of a more loyal purpose '. Note the sneer at some of the governing class. The **quamquam** clause is a corrective, ' though they are really . . .'.

l. 13. **motus conatusque,** ' risings and attempts ', perhaps an hendiadys for ' attempted risings '.

l. 16. **atque adeo,** ' or rather '.

l. 17. **vestrum,** genitive pl., (partitive) depending on **omnium.**

l. 20. **cui,** dative of **quis** = ' anyone ' after **si, nisi, num, ne.**

l. 20. **solutior,** comparative, ' too lax '; ' too weak '.

l. 20. **hoc exspectavit,** ' has (only) waited for this '.

l. 21. **quod reliquum est,** ' as to what is remaining ' = ' for the future '.

l. 25. **qui** = ' any '.

l. 26. **qui** = ' whosoever '.

l. 26. **se . . . commoverit,** *lit.,* ' will have moved himself ' = ' makes a move '.

l. 29. **egregios,** ' excellent '.

l. 31. **carcerem,** ' prison (for execution) '.

l. 32. **esse voluerunt,** ' declared should be '.

CHAPTER XIII

Sections 28–29

Line 3. post hominum memoriam, *lit.,* ' after the history of men ', = ' in living memory ', to be taken closely with **crudelissimum ac maximum.**

l. 4. **me uno togato duce et imperatore,** *lit.,* ' me alone a civilian as leader and commander ' = ' under my civilian leadership and command '. Note the abl. absol. construction.

togatus, ' wearing the toga ' is often used of a civilian as opposed to a foreigner or a soldier. In the illustration on p. ĳ̊, an orator wears a tunic, visible on his breast, underneath his toga. The arm rests in a fold made by a portion of the garment which comes over the right shoulder, down in front of the breast, and is then thrown again over the left shoulder. In this way the speaker was prevented from using his right arm in too violent gesticulation.

l. 5. **sedetur,** from sedo (1).

l. 8. **vis,** a noun. ' violence '; ' force '.

l. 9. **me . . . de hac . . . lenitate deduxerint,** ' will have led me from this leniency of purpose ' = ' make me withdraw from this position of leniency '.

l. 11. **quod,** ' which '.

l. 11. **in tanto et tam insidioso bello,** ' in so great and so dangerous a war ' = ' in such a terrible and dangerous war '.

l. 11. **optandum,** ' possible to desire '. In negative sentences, the gerundive often has the idea of *possibility*, rather than of necessity.

l. 12. **neque . . . et,** ' not only not . . . but also '.

l. 12. **poena,** ablative.

l. 16. **non dubiis,** ' not doubtful ' = ' certain *or* sure '. Note this figure of speech, known as litotes (*lit.*, ' frugality ') whereby emphasis is obtained by using a combination of the negative + the opposite of what is intended.

l. 17. **quibus ducibus,** abl. absol., ' whom (as) guides ' = ' under whose guidance '.

l. 18. **non procul . . . sed hic praesentes,** ' not afar off . . . but here being present (= by their real presence) '.

procul, i.e. on the field of battle where the enemy have often been defeated.

l. 19. **ab,** ' from '.

l. 22. **quam urbem . . . voluerunt, hanc . . . defendant.** Order for translation : **defendant hanc urbem quam,** etc. Note the position of **urbem** inside the relative clause.

l. 23. **voluerunt,** ' have destined '. For this meaning, compare **voluerunt,** Chap. XII, l. 32.

VOCABULARY

In the following Vocabulary only irregular verbs are given their principal parts in full. Otherwise the figures (1), (2), (3), (4), denote that it is a regular example of that conjugation.

The Roman and Arabic numerals attached to meanings refer to the First or Second Speech and the Sections of them.

A

a, ab, abs, *with abl.,* from ; by.

abeo, -ire, -ii, -itum, go away, depart, retire.

abhorreo (2), have no share in (I, 18) ; be contrary to (I, 20).

abicio, -ere, -ieci, -iectum, throw away, cast down.

abs = ab.

absum, -esse, afui, am far from, absent from.

abundantia, -ae, *f.,* abundance.

abutor, -i, -usus sum, *with abl.,* abuse, outrage.

ac = atque.

accedo, -ere, -cessi, -cessum, draw near, approach.

accelero (1), hurry.

accido, -ere, -cidi, happen.

accubo (1), recline.

accuso (1), accuse.

acer, -cris, -cre, keen, eager ; severe.

acerbus, -a, -um, bitter.

acies, -ei, *f.,* edge (*of weapon*) ; line (*of battle*).

acriter, *adv.,* keenly, eagerly.

ad, *with acc.,* to, towards ; near, by ; at the house of (I, 19) ;

with a view to ; **ad caedem,** for death.

adduco, -ere, -duxi, -ductum, induce, lead on.

adeo, *adv.,* even, actually.

adfectus, -a, -um, worn out.

adfero, -ferre, attuli, adlatum, bring *or* carry to ; cause.

adficio, -ere, -feci, -fectum, visit (*with punishment*) ; punish.

adflicto (1), distress, torment.

adfligo, -ere, -flixi, -flictum, throw down ; harass, dishearten.

adgrego (1), assemble.

adhibeo, -ere, -hibui, -hibitum, employ, use.

adhuc, *adv.,* hitherto, as yet.

adipiscor -i, adeptus, obtain, win.

adiuvo, -are, -iuvi, -iutum, help, assist.

administer, -stri, *m.,* assistant, helper.

administro (1), govern.

admirandus, -a, -um, wonderful, admirable.

admiror (1), wonder at, admire.

adparatus, -a, -um, lavish.

adquiro, -ere, -quisivi, -quisitum, gain.

adsequor, -i, -secutus sum, attain.
adservo (1), keep in charge.
adsido, -ere, -sedi, sit down, take one's seat.
adspectus, -us, m., sight.
adsuefacio, -ere, -feci, -factum, accustom.
adsum, -esse, adfui, be present or near.
adulescens, -ntis, c., young man.
adulescentulus, -a, -um, weak, feeble youth.
adulter, -eri, m., adulterer.
adultus, -a, -um, full grown, fully developed.
adventus, -us, m., approach, arrival.
aedes, -is, f., temple.
aedificium, n., in pl., property.
aedifico (1) build.
aeger, -gra, -grum, sick.
aequitas, -tatis, f., justice, fairness.
aequus, -a, -um, fair, just; aequo animo, with fortitude.
aerarium, -i, n., exchequer, treasury.
aes alienum, aeris alieni, n., debt.
aestus, -us, m., heat.
aetas, -tatis, f., age.
aeternus, -a, -um, eternal.
ager, agri, m., territory ; in pl., fields, lands.
agnosco, -ere, -gnovi, -gnitum, recognise.
ago, -ere, egi, actum, do ; agere cum, plead with.
agrestis, -e, as noun, countryman ; as adj., boorish.
Ahala, -ae, m., C. Servilius Ahala.
aio, ait, aiunt, defect. verb, say, assert.
alea, -ae, f., gambling.

aleator, -oris, m., gambler.
alienus, -i, m., stranger, foreigner.
aliquando, adv., at some time or other ; one day ; with imperat., at length, now at last.
aliqui, -qua, -quod, indef. adj., some, any.
aliquis, -qua, -quid, indef. pron., someone, something ; anyone, anything.
aliquo, adv., to some place ; somewhere.
aliquot, indeclin., several.
alius, -a, -ud, another, other.
alo, -ere, -ui, altum, feed, support.
altaria, -ium, n. pl., altar.
alter, -era, -erum, the one, the other (of two).
amentia, -ae, f., madness, frenzy.
amictus, -a, -um, perf. part. pass. of amicio, covered, wrapped.
amicus, -i, m., friend.
amo (1), be fond of, like, love ; desire.
amor, -oris, m., desire, lust.
amplius, adv., more, besides.
amplus, -a, -um, distinguished.
an, conj., or, whether.
angulus, -i, m., corner.
anhelo (1), breathe out (transit.).
animadverto, -ere, -ti, -sum, observe ; punish (I, 30).
animus, -i, m., mind, feeling, purpose, intention.
annus, -i, m., year.
ante, prep. with acc., and adv., before ; before, previously.
antea, adv., before, previously.
antelucanus, -a, -um, lasting all night.
antiquus, -a, -um, ancient, old.
Apenninus, -i, m., the Apennines.

aperte, *adv.*, openly.

apertus, -a, -um, open.

appello (1), address, speak to.

appropinquo (1), approach.

apud, *prep. with acc.*, at the house of.

Apulia, -ae, *f.*, Apulia (*district in South-East Italy*).

aqua, -ae, *f.*, water.

aquila, ae, *f.*, eagle.

arbitror (1), believe, think, consider.

arceo, -ere, -cui, arctum, keep *or* ward off, repel.

ardeo, -ere, arsi, arsum, be in flames, burn.

argenteus, -a, -um, of silver.

argentum, -i, *n.*, (silver) plate.

arma, -orum, *n. pl.*, arms, in armis, under arms.

armatus, -a, -um, armed ; *as noun*, armed man.

ascisco, -ere, -scivi, -scitum, enroll.

aspicio, -ere, -spexi, -spectum, look at.

at, *conj.*, but, yet.

atque *or* ac, and also, and.

atrox, -ocis, savage.

attendo, -ere, -tendi, -tentum, *with or without* animum, mark, observe.

attribuo, -ere, -tribui, -tributum, assign, allot.

auctionarius, -a, -um, of an auction ; tabulae auction-ariae, catalogue of goods to be sold by auction.

auctor, -oris, *m.*, creator, author.

auctoritas, -tatis, *f.*, resolution (*of the senate*) ; power, authority ; influence.

audacia, -ae, *f.*, insolence, effron-tery.

audax, -acis, bold, insolent.

audeo, -ere, ausus sum, *semi-dep.*, venture, dare.

audio (4), hear.

Aurelia Via, -ae, *f.*, the Via Aurelia, Aurelian Road.

Aurelium Forum, -i, *n.*, a small town in Etruria.

auris, -is, *f.*, ear.

auspicium, -i, *n.*, augury, aus-pices.

aut, *conj.*, or ; aut . . . aut, either . . . or

autem, *conj.*, on the other hand, now, moreover.

auxilium, -i, *n.*, aid, help, assis-tance.

avus, -i, *m.*, grandfather.

B

bacchor (1), revel.

barbatus, -a, -um, (having a beard), bearded.

beatus, -a, -um, happy, fortu-nate ; well to do, wealthy.

bellum, -i, *n.*, war.

bene (*adv. of* bonus), well.

beneficium, -i, *n.*, kindness.

bibo, -ere, bibi, drink.

bona, -orum, *n. pl.*, goods, pro-perty.

bonus, -a, -um, good ; patriotic ; boni, -orum, *m. pl.*, loyal citi-zens, patriots, the conservative party.

brevis, -e, short.

C

C., *abbreviation for* Caius, Gaius, a Roman praenomen.

caedes, -is, *f.*, murder.

caelum, -i, *n.*, sky.

calamitas, -tatis, *f.*, misfortune.

Campus, -i, Martius, -i, *m.*, the Campus Martius (*in Rome*).

canto (1), sing.

capillus, -i, *m.*, hair.

capio, -ere, cepi, captum, take ; suffer (*of harm*) ; contain (II, 22) ; form (*a plan*).

capitalis, -e, deadly.

carcer, -eris, *m.*, prison.

careo (2), *with abl.*, be deprived of, go without.

carus, -a, -um, dear.

castra, -orum, *n. pl.*, camp, encampment.

casus, -us, *m.*, chance, accident.

Catilina, -ae, *m.*, L. Sergius Catiline.

causa, -ae, *f.*, cause, reason ; *abl.*, causa *with gen. preceding*, for the sake of.

cedo, -ere, cessi, cessum, yield, give way to.

cena, -ae, *f.*, dinner.

centurio, -ionis, *m.*, centurion.

certamen, -inis, *n.*, contest, struggle.

certe, *adv.*, certainly, assuredly.

certo (1), strive, struggle.

certus, -a, -um, certain, sure ; certior fio, fieri, factus sum, (*lit.*, be made surer), be informed, be told.

ceterus, -a, -um, *in pl.*, the rest.

cibus, -i, *m.*, food.

Cicero, -onis, *m.*, M. Tullius Cicero.

cinis, -eris, *m.*, ashes.

circumcludo, -ere, -cludi, -clusum, hem in, beset.

circumscriptor, -oris, *m.*, defrauder, cheat.

circumsto, -stare, -steti, stand around, surround.

civis, -is, *c.*, citizen, fellow-citizen.

civitas, -tatis, *f.*, state, country.

clamo (1), shout out.

clarus, -a, -um, clear ; famous, illustrious.

clemens, -ntis, merciful.

coepi, -isse, coeptum, began.

coerceo (2), control, curb.

coetus, -us, *m.*, meeting, assembly.

cogitatio, -ionis, *f.*, purpose, design, project.

cogito (1), think of, plan, devise.

cognosco, -ere, -gnovi, -gnitum, get to know, ascertain.

cogo, -ere, coegi, coactum, compel.

cohors, -rtis, *f.*, retinue, troop.

colligo, -ere, -legi, -lectum, collect.

colloco (1), set, station.

colonia, -ae, *f.*, colony, settlement.

colonus, -i, *m.*, colonist.

comes, -itis, *c.*, companion, comrade.

comissatio, -ionis, *f.*, revelry.

comitatus, -a, -um (*perf. part. pass. of* comito), attended, accompanied.

comitia, -orum, *n. pl.*, assembly ; elections (I, 11).

comitium, -i, *n.*, a place of meeting, *esp.* by the Roman Forum where the assemblies were held, the comitium.

commemoro (1), declare.

commendatio, -ionis, *f.*, recommendation.

commissum, -i, *n.*, an offence, a crime.

committo, -ere, -misi, -missum, commit, perpetrate (*a crime*).

commoveo, -ere, -movi, -motum, move (*transit.*) ; *reflexively* (I, 6 ; II, 27) =move (*intransit.*) ; alarm (I, 22).

communis, -e, common.

comparo (1), prepare.

comperio, -ire, -peri, -pertum, ascertain, learn.

competitor, -oris, *m.*, candidate.

complector, -i, -plexus, embrace, hold in one's arms.

complexus, -us, *m.*, embrace.

complures, -ium, several, very many.

comprehendo, -ere, -ndi, -nsum, arrest.

comprimo, -ere, -pressi, -pressum, crush.

conatus, -us, *m.*, effort, attempt.

concedo, -ere, -cessi, -cessum, withdraw ; grant, concede.

concido, -ere, -cidi, collapse.

concipio, -ere, -cepi, -ceptum, conceive, imagine.

concito (1), arouse, stir up.

concordia, -ae, *f.*, harmony.

concupisco, -ere, -cupivi, -cupitum, desire eagerly.

concursus, -us, *m.*, gathering.

condemno (1), sentence, condemn.

condicio, -ionis, *f.*, vocation, task.

confectus, *see* conficio.

confero, -ferre, -tuli, collatum, bring together, compare ; se conferre, betake oneself ; conferre pestem, to bring a scourge (upon someone) from all sides.

confertus, -a, -um, stuffed, filled with.

confestim, *adv.*, immediately.

conficio, -ere, -feci, -fectum, destroy, weaken ; *esp. in perf.*

part. pass., confectus, weakened, impaired.

confido, -ere, -fisus sum, *semidep.*, be confident that, trust.

confirmo (1), strengthen, confirm ; declare.

conflagro (1), be consumed.

confligo, -ere, -flixi, -flictum, fight.

conflo (1), weld (I, 25) ; rouse (*unpopularity*) (I, 23).

congregor (1), flock together, assemble.

conicio, -ere, -ieci, -iectum, direct (*an attack*) ; drive (II, 1).

coniungo, -ere, -nxi, -nctum, unite, link.

coniuratio, -ionis, *f.*, conspiracy, plot ; the conspirators.

coniuratus, -i, *m.*, conspirator.

coniveo, -ere, -nixi, overlook, connive at.

conor (1), endeavour, attempt, try.

consceleratus, -a, -um, wicked, depraved ; *as noun*, wretch, villain.

conscientia, -ae, *f.*, consciousness.

conscriptus, -a, -um, *esp.* patres conscripti, conscript fathers, (*title of the senate*).

consensio, -ionis, *f.*, unanimity.

consequor, -i, -secutus sum, catch up, gain.

conservo (1), preserve, save.

consilium, -i, *n.*, plan, plot ; counsel ; council (I, 2).

conspicio, -ere, -spexi, -spectum, look at.

constantia, -ae, *f.*, constancy, firmness (*of character*) ; resolution.

constituo, -ere, -stitui, -stitutum, erect; appoint, settle; mark out (*for slaughter*) (I, 16).

constringo, -ere, -inxi, -ictum, restrain, fetter.

consul, -ulis, *m.*, consul.

consularis, -e, consular; *as a noun*, an ex-consul, man of consular rank.

consulatus, -us, *m.*, consulship, consulate.

consulo, -ere, -ului, -ultum, consult, ask the advice of (*with acc.*); consult the interests of (*with dat.*), II, 26.

consultum, -i, *n.*, decision; decree (*of the senate*).

consumo, -ere, -sumpsi, -sumptum, spend.

contamino (1), sully.

contemno, -ere, -tempsi, -temptum, despise.

contendo, -ere, -di, -ntum, contrast.

contentus, -a, -um, satisfied.

continentia, -ae, *f.*, self-control.

contineo, -ere, -ui, -tentum, check, restrain; keep within (I, 6); *in pass.*, live (I, 19).

contingo, -ere, -tigi, -tactum, happen.

contra, *adv.*, and *prep. with acc.*, against.

contraho, -ere, -traxi, -tractum, contract, incur.

controversia, -ae, *f.*, quarrel, dispute.

contumelia, -ae, *f.*, invective.

convenio, -ire, -veni, -ventum, meet; convenit, *impers.*, it is agreed, it is fitting.

conventus, -us, *m.*, meeting.

converto, -ere, -ti, -sum, change.

convinco, -ere, -vici, -victum, prove wrong, convict.

convivium, -i, *n.*, banquet.

convoco (1), summon together, assemble, convene.

copia, -ae, *f.*, abundance, plenty; copiae, -arum, *pl.*, forces, troops.

copiosus, -a, -um, well-supplied with, rich in.

corpus, -oris, *n.*, body.

corrigo, -ere, -rexi, -rectum, amend, improve.

corroboro (1), strengthen.

corruo, -ere, -ui, fall, collapse.

corruptela, -ae, *f.*, corruption, bribery.

corruptor, -oris, *m.*, seducer.

corruptus, -a, -um, corrupt; *as noun*, corrupt man.

cotidie, *adv.*, daily, every day.

credo, -ere, -didi, -ditum, believe; (*ironically*), suppose (I, 5).

cresco, -ere, crevi, cretum, grow, increase.

crudelis, -e, cruel.

crudeliter, *adv.*, cruelly.

cruentus, -a, -um, bloody, bloodstained.

culpa, -ae, *f.*, fault.

cum, *with abl.*, with, together with.

cum, *conj.*, when; since; although.

cumulo (1), augment, increase.

cunctus, -a, -um, all.

cupiditas, -tatis, *f.*, desire; passion.

cupio, -ere, -ivi *or* -ii, -itum, desire, want.

cur, why.

cura, -ae, *f.*, care.

curia, -ae, the Senate House.

cursus, -us, *m.*, course.
custodia, -ae, *f.*, custody (I, 19) ;
in *pl.*, guards, sentinels.
custodio (4), watch over, guard.
custos, -odis, *c.*, guardian, guard.

D

de, *with abl.*, down from ; about,
concerning.
debeo (2), must, ought.
debilito (1), weaken.
debitus, -a, -um, (*perf. part. pass.
of* debeo), due, deserved.
decerno, -ere, -crevi, -cretum,
decide, decree.
declinatio, -ionis, *f.*, side turn (*of
the body*).
decoctor, -oris, *m.*, spendthrift,
bankrupt.
dedecus, -oris, *n.*, disgrace ; infamy.
deduco, -ere, -duxi, -ductum,
bring ; lead away from (II, 18,
28).
defatigatus, -a, -um, worn out,
exhausted.
defendo, -ere, -ndi, -nsum, defend.
defero, -ferre, -tuli, -latum, report
(*to the senate*).
deficio, -ere, -feci, -fectum, desert,
withdraw one's allegiance from
(I, 28) ; fail.
defigo, -ere, -xi, -xum, lodge *or*
fix in.
deinde, *adv.*, thereafter, then.
delecto (1), delight.
deleo, -ere, -levi, -letum, destroy.
delicatus, -a, -um, effeminate.
deligo, -ere, -legi, -lectum, pick
out, choose.
demigro (1), depart ; move on
(I, 19).

demonstro (1), point out, show,
prove.
denique, *adv.*, finally, in short ; at
last.
depello, -ere, -puli, -pulsum,
drive away.
depono, -ere, -posui, -positum,
set *or* lay aside.
deposco, -ere, -poposci, demand,
claim.
deprecor (1), avert by prayer,
seek to avoid.
deprehendo, -ere, -di, -sum, catch,
seize.
derelictus, -a, -um, bankrupt
(*lit.*, abandoned, deserted).
derelinquo, -ere, -liqui, -lictum,
abandon completely, desert.
describo, -ere, -scripsi, -scriptum,
describe.
desero, -ere, -serui, -sertum,
abandon, forsake, desert.
desiderium, -i, *n.*, longing (for).
desidero (1), long for.
designo (1) single out. designatus,
-a, -um, (magistrate) elect.
desino, -ere, -sii, -situm, cease.
desisto, -ere, -stiti, -stitum, cease.
desperatio, -ionis, *f.*, despair.
desperatus, -a, -um, hopeless,
desperate.
despero (1), despair (of).
desum, -esse, -fui, (*usually with
dat.*) be wanting to ; fail.
detestor (1), remove (*by prayer*) ;
escape.
detraho, -ere, -traxi, -tractum,
take away, remove.
detrimentum, -i, *n.*, harm.
deus, -i, *m., god ; n. pl.*, dei *or* di ;
abl. pl., deis, dis.
devoveo, -ere, -vovi, -votum,
consecrate, vow, devote.

dextera (dextra), -ae, f., right hand.

dico, -ere, -xi, -ctum, say, speak.

dictator, -oris, m., dictator.

dictatura, -ae, f., dictatorship.

dictito (1), declare, maintain, assert.

dies, -ei, m., day; in dies singulos, every day, daily.

difficultas, -tatis, f., difficulty; (money) difficulties, reduced circumstances (I, 14).

dignus, -a, -um, with abl., worthy of.

dilectus, -us, m., levy (of troops); choice, selection.

diligens, -ntis, careful, watchful.

diligenter, adv., carefully.

diligentia, -ae, f., watchfulness, vigilance.

dimitto, -ere, -misi, -missum, dismiss.

direptio, -ionis, f., pillaging, plundering.

direptor, -oris, m., pillager, plunderer.

discedo, -ere, -cessi, -cessum, depart, be gone.

discessus, -us, m., departure.

disciplina, -ae, f., training, discipline.

disco, -ere, didici, learn.

discribo, -ere, -psi, -ptum, distribute, apportion.

dissimilis, -e, different, unlike.

dissimulo (1), hide, conceal.

dissolutus, -a, -um, remiss, neglectful (of duty).

dissolvo, -ere, -solvi, -solutum, dissolve, free from debt.

distribuo, -ere, -ui, -utum, divide out, distribute.

diu, adv., for a long time or while; long; comp., diutius, longer, (any) longer.

divello, -ere, -velli, -vulsum, tear (apart or away).

diversus, -a, -um, different.

do, dare, dedi, datum, give.

dolor, -oris, m., pain, grief.

domesticus, -a, -um, private, domestic; (of war) civil.

dominatio, -ionis, f., power.

domus, -us, f., house, home; loc., domi, at home.

dormio (4), sleep.

dubito (1), hesitate.

dubium, -i, n., doubt.

dubius, -a, -um, doubtful.

duco, -ere, -xi, -ctum, lead.

dudum, adv., some time since or ago; iam dudum, this long time.

duint = dent, pres. subj. act. of do.

dum, conj., while; with subj., so long as, provided that.

duo, -ae, -o, two.

dux, ducis, c., leader.

E

ebrius, -a, -um, drunk; as noun, drunkard.

ecquis, -quid, interrog. pron., is there anyone? any? anybody?

edictum, -i, n., edict.

edoceo, -ere, -ui, -ctum, inform, show.

educo, -ere, -xi, -ctum, lead out or forth, take.

effero, -ferre, extuli, elatum, carry forth (II, 2); promote (I, 28).

effrenatus, -a, -um, unbridled, unrestrained.

effugio, -ere, -fugi, flee away, escape from.

egens, -ntis, needy.

egeo, *with abl.,* lack, need.

egestas, -tatis, *f.,* need, necessity, want.

ego, I.

egredior, -i, -gressus, go out, leave.

egregius, -a, -um, excellent, eminent.

eicio, -ere, -ieci, -iectum, expel ; **se eicere,** fling oneself forth.

eius modi, of that kind = such a.

elabor, -i, -lapsus, slip away *or* from.

eludo, -ere, -si, -sum, baffle ; mock.

emergo, -ere, -si, -sum, extricate *or* free oneself ; get clear.

emitto, -ere, -misi, -missum, send forth.

emorior, -i, -mortuus, die off, die.

enim, *conj.,* for.

eo, *adv.,* thither, there, to that place.

eo, ire, ivi *or* **ii, itum,** go.

eodem, *adv.,* to the same place.

eques, -itis, *m.,* horseman, knight ; **equites,** the Knights, the Equestrian Party.

ergo, *adv.,* then, therefore, so then.

eripio, -ere, -ripui, -reptum, take away ; snatch *or* rescue from.

erro (1), be wrong *or* mistaken.

eructo, (1), belch forth, vomit.

erumpo, -ere, -rupi, -ruptum, burst forth *or* in ; burst out upon (I, 31) ; be disclosed (I, 6).

et, and ; **et . . . et,** both . . . and.

etenim, *conj.,* and *or* for indeed.

etiam, *conj.,* also ; even ; still ; **etiam atque etiam,** again and again, repeatedly.

Etruria, -ae, *f.,* Etruria (*district north of Rome and the Tiber*).

evado, -ere, -di, -sum, go out, depart.

everto, -ere, -ti, -sum, overthrow.

evocator, -oris, *m.,* summoner, recruiter, one who calls up.

evomo, -ere, -ui, -itum, (vomit forth) ; expel, disgorge.

e *or* **ex,** *with abl.,* out of, from ; in accordance with.

exaudio (4), hear clearly.

excedo, -ere, -cessi, -cessum, go out, leave.

excido, -ere, -cidi, fall out of *or* from.

excito (1), arouse.

excludo, -ere, -si, -sum, shut out ; refuse admission to (I, 10).

excogito (1), think out, plan.

excursio, -ionis, *f.,* inroad, expedition, invasion.

exeo, -ire, -ivi *or* **-ii, -itum,** go out *or* forth, leave, depart.

exerceo (2), train.

exercitatio, -ionis, *f.,* training, practice.

exercitus, -us, *m.,* army.

exhaurio, -ire, -hausi, -haustum, (drain out), remove.

existimo (1), think, consider.

exitium, -i, *n.,* destruction, ruin.

exsilium, -i, *n.,* banishment, exile.

expello, -ere, -puli, -pulsum, drive out.

expono, -ere, -posui, -positum, set forth, explain.

expromo, -ere, -psi, -ptum, exhibit, display.

exsisto, -ere, -stiti, -stitum, appear, arise (I, 18) ; be, exist (I, 14).

exspecto (1), expect, wait for.

exstinguo, -ere, -nxi, -nctum, put out, quench, extinguish.

exsul, -ulis, m., exile.

exsulto (1), revel, exult, triumph ; run riot (I, 26).

externus, -a, -um, foreign.

exterus, -a, -um, foreign.

extorqueo, -ere, -torsi, -tortum, wrest from.

extra, with acc., beyond, outside.

F

facile, adv., comp. facilius, easily, readily.

facilis, -e, easy.

facinorosus, -a, -um, criminal, villainous, atrocious.

facinus, -oris, n., crime, villainy.

facio, -ere, feci, factum, make, do ; satis facio, with dat., satisfy ; pass., fio, be made, become.

factum, -i, n., deed.

Faesulanus, -a, -um, of Faesulae, (town in N. Italy).

falcarius, -i, m., scythe or sickle-maker.

fallo, -ere, fefelli, falsum, deceive.

falsus, -a, -um, false, groundless.

fama, -ae, f., reputation.

fames, -is, f., hunger.

familia, -ae, f., household.

familiariter, adv., sup., familiaris-sime, on the most intimate or friendly terms.

fasces, -ium, m. pl., the fasces (bundle of rods with an axe).

fateor, -eri, fassus, confess, admit.

fatum, -i, n., fate, doom.

fauces, -ium, f. pl., jaw (II, 2) ; narrow pass, defile (I, 5).

fax, facis, f., torch, firebrand.

febris, -is, f., fever.

fero, ferre, tuli, latum, carry ; endure ; receive (an answer) (I, 19) ; report ; talk of (I, 26).

ferrum, -i, n., sword.

fides, -is, f., credit ; good faith.

fingo, -ere, -inxi, -ctum, imagine.

finis, -is, m., boundary, limit ; quem ad finem, till when. how long? in pl., territory.

fio, fieri, factus sum, pass. of facio, am made, or done, become.

firmo (1), strengthen.

firmus, -a, -um, firm, strong.

Flaccus, -i, m., M. Fulvius Flac-cus.

flagitiosissime, superl. adv., (flagi-tiose) ; most shamefully or infamously.

flagitiosus, -a, -um, shameful, infamous, dissolute.

flagitium, -i, n., a shameful deed, wickedness, scandalous vice.

flagito (1), demand.

flamma, -ae, f., fire, blaze.

florens, -ntis, prosperous.

flos, -oris, m., flower, pick, best part.

foedus, -eris, n., alliance, league.

foras, adv., out of doors ; out.

fore, fut. infin. of sum.

foris, adv., out of doors, abroad, without.

fortasse, adv., perhaps.

fortis, -e, strong, brave, gallant.

fortitudo, -inis, f., bravery ; firm-ness (I, 28).

fortuna, -ae, f., fortune, fate.

fortunatus, -a, -um, fortunate, happy.

forum, -i, n., the forum (in Rome).

Forum Aurelium, -i, n., small town in Etruria.

frango, -ere, fregi, fractum, break; **te frangere,** break your resolution (I, 22).

fraudatio, -ionis, *f.,* cheating, deceit, fraud.

frequentia, -ae, *f.,* crowded meeting, large numbers (I, 21).

fretus, -a, -um, *with abl.,* relying on.

frigus, -oris, *n.,* cold.

frons, -ntis, *f.,* forehead.

fructus, -us, *m.,* enjoyment; produce (II, 18).

fuga, -ae, *f.,* flight; exile.

fugitivus, -i, *m.,* runaway slave.

fulgeo, -ere, -lsi, gleam, shine.

Fulvius, -i, *m.,* M. Fulvius Flaccus.

funestus, -a, -um, deadly.

furiosus, -a, -um, mad, frantic.

furo (3), rage, rave, be mad *or* frantic.

furor, -oris, *m.,* madness, frenzy.

futurus, -a, -um, *future participle of* sum.

G

Gallicanus, -a, -um, Gallic.

Gallicus, -a, -um, Gallic.

ganeo, -eonis, *m.,* glutton, debauchee.

gaudium, -i, *n.,* joy, delight.

gelidus, -a, -um, cold.

gens, -ntis, *f.,* race: *in pl.,* mankind.

genus, -eris, *n.,* kind, class, type.

gero, -ere, gessi, gestum, do; (*of war*) wage.

gladiator, -oris, *m.,* gladiator; ruffian.

gladiatorius, -a, -um, gladiatorial.

gladius, -i, *m.,* sword.

gloria, -ae, *f.,* glory, renown.

Gracchus, -i, *m.,* (1) Tiberius Gracchus. (2) C. Gracchus.

gradus, -us, *m.,* grade, degree.

gratia, -ae, *f.,* thankfulness, gratitude, thanks.

gravis, -e, weighty; grievous, dreadful.

graviter, *adv.,* severely.

grex, gregis, *f.,* band, troop, clique.

H

habeo (2), have; deliver (*of a speech*); hold (*a meeting of the senate*); feel (gratitude) (I, 11).

habito (1), live.

haereo, -ere, -si, -sum, be attached to.

haesito (1), hesitate, be irresolute.

hebesco (3), grow dull *or* blunt.

hesternus, -a, -um, of yesterday; dies h., yesterday.

hic, haec, hoc, *demonstr. pron.,* this, this here; he, she, it, they.

hic, *adv.,* in this place, here.

hinc, *adv.,* from this place; *in contrast to* illinc =on this side, here.

hisce, old form of his. See hic.

homo, -inis, *c.,* a human being; man.

honestas, -tatis, *f.,* uprightness, integrity, virtue.

honeste, *adv.,* nobly, virtuously.

honesto (1), make honourable.

honestus, -a, -um, respected, distinguished.

honor, -oris, *m.,* public honour, office.

hora, -ae, *f.,* an hour.

horribilis, -e, terrible, dreadful.

hortor (1), encourage, exhort, urge.

hostis, -is, c., enemy.

huc, adv., hither, to this point.

huiusce, old form of huius. See hic.

humanus, -a, -um, human.

humus, -i, f., ground; loc., humi, on the ground.

I

iaceo (2), lie.

iacto (1), throw; se iactare, swagger; in pass., toss about (I, 31).

iam, now, already; nunc iam, at this very time; iam diu, for a long time past; iam pridem, long ago, long since.

Ianuarius, -a, -um, of January.

idcirco, adv., on that account, therefore.

idem, eadem, idem, the same.

Idus, -uum, f. pl., the Ides.

igitur, therefore.

ignavia, -ae, f., idleness, sloth; cowardice.

ignominia, -ae, f., disgrace, infamy.

ignoro (1), not know.

ille, -a, -ud, demonstr. pron., that; he, she, it, they.

illecebra, -ae, f., enticement, allurement.

illinc, adv., from that place; in contrast to hinc = on that side, there.

illustro (1), bring to light; explain.

imberbis, -e, beardless.

immanitas, -tatis, f., enormity.

immineo (2), impend, threaten; (lit., overhang).

immitto, -ere, -misi, -missum, send in, into or against.

immo, adv., on the contrary, nay.

immortalis, -e, immortal.

impedio (4), hinder, prevent.

impello, -ere, -puli, -pulsum, urge, drive on.

impendeo (2), hang over; with dat., threaten.

imperator, -oris, m., commander-in-chief, general.

imperitus, -a, -um, not knowing; ignorant, fool (I, 30).

imperium, -i, n., supreme power, consular authority; empire (I, 33, II, 19).

impero (1), with. dat., order, command, bid.

impetro (1), obtain (requests).

impetus, -us, m., attack, assault.

impius, -a, -um, wicked, impious.

imploro (1), beseech, implore.

importunus, -a, -um, (unsuitable), harsh, unbridled.

improbitas, -tatis, f., wickedness, depravity.

improbus, -a, -um, wicked, shameless: as noun, scoundrel, knave.

impudens, -ntis, shameless.

impudicus, -a, -um, shameless, unchaste.

impunitus, -a, -um, unpunished.

impurus, -a, -um, impure, infamous, abandoned, vile.

in, with acc., into, on to, against; with abl., in, on.

inanis, -e, empty.

incendium, -i, n., burning, conflagration, fire; caede atque incendiis, with fire and sword.

inceptus, -us, m., undertaking.

incido, -ere, -cidi, fall into, incur.

includo, -ere, -cludi, -clusum, enclose, confine.

incolumis, -e, safe, unharmed.

incredibilis, -e, incredible, inconceivable.

increpo, -are, -crepui, -crepitum, be noised abroad (I, 18) ; utter aloud.

indemnatus, -a, -um, uncondemned, unsentenced.

indico, -ere, -xi, -ctum, declare (*of war*).

induco, -ere, -xi, -ctum, (lead into) ; *with* animum, bring one's mind to, bring oneself to.

industria, -ae, *f.*, diligence, zeal, hard work.

ineo, -ire, -ii, -itum, enter ; with consilium, form a plot *or* plan.

iners, -rtis, inactive, indolent.

inertia, -ae, *f.*, inactivity, indolence, remissness.

infamis, -e, disreputable, notorious.

inferi, -orum, *m. pl.*, the dead.

infero, -ferre, -tuli, -latum, cause ; *with* manus, lay hands upon ; *with* bellum, make war upon.

infestus, -a, -um, hostile, dangerous.

infitiator, -oris, *m.*, shirker, debtor.

infitior (1), deny, disown.

inflammo (1), set on fire.

ingens, -ntis, huge, vast.

ingravesco (3), grow heavier *or* worse.

ingredior, -i, -gressus, enter upon, begin.

inimicitia, -ae, *f.*, enmity, hostility.

inimicus, -i, *m.*, unfriendly, hostile ; *as noun*, enemy, foe.

iniquitas, -tatis, *f.*, unfairness, injustice.

iniquus, -a, -um, unfair, unjust.

initio (1), initiate.

iniuria, -ae, *f.*, wrong ; *abl.*, iniuria, unjustly, undeservedly.

inlustro (1) bring to light, explain.

innocens, -ntis, guiltless, innocent.

inopia, -ae, *f.*, need.

inquam, -is, -it, say.

inscribo, -ere, -psi, -ptum, write in *or* on ; inscribe.

insidiae, -arum, *f. pl.*, ambush, plot.

insidiator, -oris, *m.*, waylayer, plotter.

insidior (1), lie in wait for ; plot against (*with dat.*).

insidiosus, -a, -um, treacherous, dangerous.

insolenter, *adv.*, *comp.* insolentius, haughtily, insolently.

insperatus, -a, -um, unlooked for, unexpected.

insto, -are, -stiti, press upon, harass, menace.

instrumentum, -i, *n.*, in *pl.*, resources, means.

instruo, -ere, -uxi, -uctum, draw up.

intellego, -ere, -lexi, -lectum, perceive, understand, know.

intendo, -ere, -di, -tum, intend, purpose.

inter, *with acc.*, between, among ; inter se, to one another.

intercedo, -ere, -cessi, -cessum, intervene, pass (*of time*).

intereo, -ire, -ii, -itum, perish.

interficio, -ere, -feci, -fectum, put to death, murder.

interitus, -us, *m.*, destruction, death.

interrogo (1), question, ask.

intersum, -esse, -fui, be *or* lie between.

intestinus, -a, -um, internal; (*of war*), civil.

intimus, -i, *m.*, intimate (*friend*).

intra, *with acc.*, within, inside.

intus, *adv.*, within.

inuro, -ere, -ussi, -ustum, burn in, brand on.

invenio, -ire, -veni, -ventum, come upon, find.

invictus, -a, -um, unconquered.

invidia, -ae, *f.*, odium, unpopularity.

invidiosus, -a, -um, exciting envy *or* unpopularity, hateful, odious.

invito (1), invite, ask.

Iovi, *dat. of* Iuppiter.

ipse, -a, -um, self, very.

irretio (4), ensnare, inveigle.

is, ea, id, *demonstr. pron.*, that; he, she, it, they; id temporis (I, 10), at that time.

iste, -a, -ud, that (*of yours*); your, that; such (I, 3).

ita, *adv.*, so, thus; ita ut, in the way in which; in such a way that.

Italia, -ae, *f.*, Italy.

itaque, and so.

iter, itineris, *n.*, road, way.

iubeo, -ere, iussi, iussum, order, bid.

iucundus, -a, -um, agreeable, pleasant.

iudicium, -i, *n.*, judgment.

iudico (1), judge, consider.

iungo, -ere, -nxi, -nctum, join.

Iuppiter, Iovis, *m.*, Jupiter, Jove.

ius, iuris, *n.*, right, justice; *pl.*, rights; *abl.*, iure, rightly, justly; iure optimo, most justly (I, 21).

iussus, -us, *m.*, order, command; iussu meo, at my bidding.

iustus, -a, -um, just, righteous; (*of an accusation*), well-grounded, merited.

iuventus, -utis, *f.*, youth.

K

Kalendae, -arum, *f. pl.*, the Kalends, (*first day of the month*).

L

L., *abbreviation for* Lucius, Roman praenomen.

labefacto (1), cause to totter, shake, weaken.

labor, -oris, *m.*, labour, toil.

Laeca, -ae, *m.*, M. Laeca, a supporter of Catiline.

laetitia, -ae, *f.*, joy, gladness.

laetor (1), rejoice, be glad.

languidus, -a, -um, languid, sluggish.

lateo (2), remain hidden *or* concealed, lurk.

latro, -onis, *m.*, bandit, robber, brigand.

latrocinium, -i, *n.*, brigandage.

latrocinor (1), plunder, be a brigand *or* bandit.

latus, -eris, *n.*, side, flank, rib.

laus, laudis, *f.*, praise; fame, reputation.

lectulus, -i, *m.*, bed.

lectus, -a, -um, picked; choice, select.

legio, -ionis, *f.*, legion.

lenis, -e, gentle, lenient.

lenitas, -tatis, *f.*, leniency.
lentus, -a, -um, tardy, indolent.
Lepidus, -i, *m.*, Manius Aemilius Lepidus.
lepidus, -a, -um, nice, effeminate.
levis, -e, inconstant, dissolute.
levo (1), lighten, relīeve, ease.
lex, legis, *f.*, law.
liber, -era, -erum, free, un-checked.
liber, libri, *m.*, book.
liberi, -orum, *m. pl.*, children.
libero (1), free, set free.
libido, -inis, *f.*, lust.
licet, (2), it is lawful, one may.
locuples, -etis, rich, wealthy, opulent.
locus, -i, *m.*, place.
longe, *adv.*, afar off, afar.
longinquus, -a, -um, distant, far-removed.
loquor, -i, locutus, speak, say.
Lucius, -i, *m.*, (*abbreviation* L.), Lucius, Roman praenomen.
ludus, -i, *m.*, school.
lugeo (2), grieve, mourn.
lux, lucis, *f.*, light ; daylight ; the light of day.
luxuria, -ae, *f.*, excess, profligacy.

M

M., *abbreviation for* Marcus, Roman praenomen.
M'., *abbreviation for* Manius, Roman praenomen.
machinor (1), contrive, devise.
macto (1), punish.
Maelius, -i, *m.*, Spurius Maelius.
maeror, -oris, *m.*, sorrow, grief.
magis, *comparat. of* magnopere, *adv.*, more.
magistratus, -us, *m.*, magistracy, magistrate.

magnifice, *adv.*, gloriously.
magno opere (*or* magnopere), *adv. of* magnus, greatly ; earnestly.
magnus, -a, -um, *comp.* maior, *superl.* maximus, great, large.
maiores, -um, *m. pl.*, ancestors, forefathers.
male, *adv.*, badly.
malleolus, -i, *m.*, fire-brand (*used in war*).
malo, malle, malui, wish rather, prefer.
malum, -i, *n.*, evil, misfortune.
mando (1), intrust, entrust ; hand over ; store (I, 27).
mane, *adv.*, in the morning.
maneo, -ere, mansi, mansum, stay, remain.
manicatus, -a, -um, with long sleeves.
manifestus, -a, -um, clear, evident.
Manlianus, -a, -um, of Manlius.
Manlius, -i, *m.*, C. Manlius, military leader of Catiline's rebellion.
manus, us, *f.*, hand ; band.
Marcellus, -i, *m.*, M. Marcellus.
mare, -is, *n.*, sea.
maritus, -i, *m.*, husband.
Marius, -i, *m.*, C. Marius.
Massilia, -ae, *f.*, Massilia (*Marseilles*).
Massiliensis, -is, of Massilia.
mature, *adv.*, *comp.* maturius, early.
maturitas, -tatis, *f.*, full growth, maturity.
maturo (1), hasten, hurry.
maxime, *superl. of* magnopere, especially, very greatly.
maximus, *superl. of* magnus.
mecum = cum me, with me.

medicina, -ae, *f.*, remedy, relief.

mediocris, -e, ordinary, mean.

mediocriter, *adv.*, moderately, slightly.

meditatus, -a, -um, *perf. part. pass. of* meditor, considered, studied.

meditor (1), purpose, contrive.

mehercule, by Hercules, assuredly.

memini, -isse (*perf. form with present meaning*) remember.

memoria, -ae, *f.*, memory, recollection.

mens, -ntis, *f.*, mind ; purpose ; reflection (I, 15) ; *in pl.*, thoughts.

mereor (2), deserve.

Metellus, -i, *m.*, (1) Q. Metellus Celer, (2) M. Metellus.

metuo, -ere, -ui, -utum, fear.

metus, -us, *m.*, fear.

meus, -a, -um, my, mine.

militaris, -e, military.

minae, -arum, *f. pl.*, threats, menaces.

minime, *adv.*, *superl. of* paulum, least, very little ; not at all.

minimus, -a, -um, *superl. of* parvus.

minister, -tri, *m.*, attendant, servant, helper.

minitor (1), threaten, menace.

minor (1), threaten, menace.

Minucius, -i, *m.*, Minucius, friend of Catiline.

minus, *adv.*, *compar. of* paulum, less.

miser, -era, -erum, wretched.

misericordia, -ae, *f.*, pity, compassion.

misericors, -rdis, merciful, pitiful.

mitis, -e, gentle, lenient, kind.

mitto, -ere, misi, missum, send.

mixtus, -a, -um, mingled, mixed, confused.

modo, *adv.* only, merely ; non modo, not only.

modus, -i, *m.*, way, manner ; huiusce (*or* eius) modi, of this kind ; nullo modo, in no way ; quodam modo, in a way.

moenia, -ium, *n. pl.*, city-walls ; city.

moles, -is, *f.*, (a mass) ; weight (*of odium*).

moleste, *adv.*, with annoyance ; moleste fero, be annoyed at.

molior (4), prepare, contrive.

mollis, -e, gentle, lenient.

moneo (2), warn, advise.

monstrum, -i, *n.*, monster.

mora, -ae, *f.*, delay.

morbus, -i, *m.*, sickness, disease.

morior, -i, mortuus, die.

mors, mortis, *f.*, death.

mortuus, -a, -um, dead.

mos, moris, *m.*, custom ; *in pl.*, ways, character, conduct ; mos maiorum (custom of one's ancestors), tradition.

motus, -us, *m.*, tumult, commotion.

moveo, -ere, movi, motum, move, affect, stir.

mucro, -onis, *m.*, blade (*of sword*).

mulier, -is, *f.*, woman.

muliercula, -ae, *f.*, common woman.

multitudo, -inis, *f.*, numbers, great *or* large numbers.

multo, *adv.*, by much ; multo magis, much more.

multo (1), punish.

multus, -a, -um, much ; *in pl.*, many.

municeps,-ipis, *c.*, citizen, burgher.
municipium, -i, *n.*, free town.
munio (4), fortify, defend.
munitus, -a, -um, fortified, secure, protected.
murus, -i, *m.*, wall.
muto (1), change, alter.

N

nam, *conj.*, for.
nanciscor, -i, nactus, get, obtain.
nascor, -i, natus, be born ; nascens (I, 30), in its infancy.
natio, -ionis, *f.*, nation, people.
natura, -ae, *f.*, nature.
naufragus, -i, *m.*, (shipwrecked person), castaway.
ne, *interj.*, truly, verily (II, 6).
ne, *conj.*, (in order) that not, lest ; *after vbs. of fearing*, lest, that.
ne, *adv.*, not ; ne ... quidem, not even.
-ne, *enclitic particle denoting a question.*
nec, *see* neque.
necem, neces, *see* nex.
necessario, *adv.*, of necessity, unavoidably.
necessarius, -i, *m.*, relative, close friend.
necesse, *indecl.*, unavoidable, necessary.
necne, or not (*in indirect questions*).
nefarie, *adv.*, wickedly, abominably.
nefarius, -a, -um, wicked, abominable.
neglego, -ere, -exi, -ectum, neglect ; set at nought (I, 18).
nego (1), say not, deny.
negotium, -i, *n.*, business.

nemo, neminem, nullius, nemini, nullo, nobody, no one.
nepos, -otis, *m.*, spendthrift.
neque (nec), *conj.*, and not, nor ; neque ... neque, neither ... nor ; neque tamen, and yet not.
nequior, *compar. of* nequam, worthless, good for nothing.
nequitia, -ae, *f.*, negligence (I, 4, 29) ; villainy (II, 11).
nescio (4), not know.
nex, necis, *f.*, death, slaughter.
nihil, *indecl.*, nothing ; *adv.*, in nothing, in no way, not at all.
nimis, nimium, *adv.*, too much, excessively, too.
nisi, *conj.*, if not, unless, except.
niteo (2), shine, glitter, look beautiful.
nitidus, -a, -um, sleek.
nix, nivis, *f.*, snow.
nobilis, -e, well-born, noble.
nobiscum = cum nobis.
nocturnus, -a, -um, at night.
nomen, -inis, *n.*, name.
nomino (1), call by name, name.
non, *adv.*, not.
nondum, *adv.*, not yet.
nonne, *interrog. adv.*, is it not? surely.
non nullus, *pl.*, non nulli, -ae, -a, some, several.
nos, we.
noster, -tra, -trum, our.
nota, -ae, *f.*, mark of infamy, disgrace.
noto (1), mark, observe.
November, -bris, -bre, of November, November.
novus, -a, -um, new ; novae res, *pl.*, revolution.
nox, noctis, *f.*, night.
nudus, -a, -um, naked, bare.

nullus, -a, -um, none, not any, no.

num, *in direct questions*, surely not; *in indirect questions*, whether, if.

numen, -inis, *n.*, (divine) power.

numerus, -i, *m.*, number.

numquam, *adv.*, never.

nunc, *adv.*, now.

nuper, *adv.*, lately.

nuptiae, -arum, *f. pl.*, marriage.

O

O, *interj.*, oh! ah!

ob, *prep. with acc.*, on account of; quam ob rem, wherefore.

obeo, -ire, -ii, -itum, commit (*a crime*).

obligo (1), pledge, mortgage.

oblitus, -a, -um, *perf. part. pass. of* oblino, bedaubed, besmeared.

obliviscor, -i, -litus, forget, be unmindful of (*with gen.*)

obscure, *adv.*, darkly, obscurely.

obscuro (1), hide, conceal.

obscurus, -a, -um, unknown.

obsideo, -ere, -sedi, -sessum, besiege, beset; lie in wait for (I, 26).

obsto, -are, -stiti, -statum, *with dat.*, withstand, oppose.

obstupefacio, -ere, -feci, -factum, astonish, amaze, benumb.

obtempero (1), *with dat.*, submit to, obey.

occido, -ere, -cidi, -cisum, slay, kill.

occultus, -a, -um, hidden, concealed, secret.

occupo (1), seize, take possession of.

oculus, -i, *m.*, eye; *in pl.*, gaze.

odi, -isse, *perf. in form, present in meaning*, hate.

odium, -i, *n.*, hatred.

offensus, -a, -um, offensive, odious, hateful.

omen, -inis, *n.*, omen.

omitto, -ere, -misi, -missum, pass over.

omnis, -e, all, every.

Opimius, -i, *m.*, Lucius Opimius, consul in 121 B.C.

opinor (1), think, suppose.

opono, -ere, -posui, -positum, set against.

oportet (2), *impersonal*, it is necessary, proper, right; one ought.

opprimo, -ere, -pressi, -pressum, overwhelm, crush, subdue.

optimates, -um (-ium) *m. pl.*, the governing class, nobles.

optimus, -a, -um (*superl. of* bonus), best, excellent.

opto (1), ask, desire.

oratio, -ionis, *f.*, speech.

orbis, -is, *m.*, *with* terrarum *or* terrae, the whole world.

ordo, -inis, *m.*, rank, class, *especially used of the senate.*

ornamentum, -i, *n.*, equipment.

ornatus, -a, -um, equipped.

os, oris, *n.*, mouth; *esp.* face.

ostendo, -ere, -di, -tum, show.

ostento (1), show; offer.

otiosus, -a, -um, at leisure; quiet.

otium, -i, *n.*, leisure; peace (I, 25).

P

P., *abbrev. for* Publius, a Roman praenomen.

paciscor, -i, pactus, agree upon.

paco (1), pacify.

pactum, -i, *n., lit.,* agreement : *in phrases* = way ; e.g. **quo pacto,** in what way? how? ; **nescio quo pacto,** *lit.,* I know not in what way = somehow or other.

pactus, -a, -um, agreed upon, settled.

paene, *adv.,* almost.

palam, *adv.,* openly.

Palatium, -i, *n.,* the Palatine Hill (*in Rome*).

parens, -ntis, *c.,* a parent.

pareo (2), *with dat.,* obey.

paries, -etis, *m.,* a wall (*of a house*) ; house (I, 19).

pario, -ere, peperi, partum, produce, beget ; win, obtain.

paro (1), make ready, prepare ; get together (I, 15).

parricida, -ae, *c.,* murderer, assassin.

parricidium, -i, *n.,* parricide.

pars, partis, *f.,* part, portion.

particeps, -cipis, *with gen.,* sharing in ; *as noun,* a sharer in.

partim . . . partim, partly . . . partly.

parum, *adv.,* too little, little.

parvus, -a, -um, small, little.

patefacio, -ere, -feci, -factum, bring to light, reveal ; *pass.* **patefio, -fieri, -factus.**

pateo (2), be open ; be exposed.

pater, patris, *m.,* father ; **patres conscripti,** the senators.

patientia, -ae, *f.,* endurance.

patior, -i, passus, bear, suffer ; allow, permit.

patria, -ae, *f.,* fatherland, native country.

patricius, -i, *m.,* nobleman, patrician.

patrimonium, -i, *m.,* inheritance, estate.

paucus, -a, -um, few, little.

paulisper, *adv.,* for a little while.

paulum, -i, *n.,* a little ; *abl.,* **paulo,** (by) a little, somewhat.

pecunia, -ae, *f.,* money.

pecus, -udis, *f.,* beast ; (*of a person*), a brute.

penitus, *adv.,* deeply.

per, *prep. with acc.,* through, by.

percello, -ere, -culi, -culsum, throw down, destroy, overthrow.

percipio, -ere, -cepi, -ceptum, perceive, observe.

perditus, -a, -um (*perf. part. pass. of* **perdo**), abandoned, dissolute, worthless.

perdo, -ere, -didi, -ditum, destroy, ruin.

pereo, -ire, -ii, -itum, perish ; be destroyed (*pass. of* **perdo**).

perfero, -ferre, -tuli, -latum, bring, bear ; endure.

perficio, -ere, -feci, -fectum, accomplish.

perfringo, -ere, -fregi, -fractum, destroy, annul.

perfruor, -i, -fructus, *with abl.,* enjoy to the full.

pergo, -ere, perrexi, perrectum, go on, proceed.

periclitor (1), risk, venture.

periculum, -i, *n.,* danger, peril.

permaneo, -ere, -mansi, -mansum, stay, remain.

permitto, -ere, -misi, -missum, entrust.

permodestus, -a, -um, very modest.

permoveo, -ere, -movi, -motum, move deeply, excite ; influence.

permulti, -ae, -a, very many.

pernicies, -ei, *f.*, destruction, ruin.

perniciosus, -a, -um, destructive, dangerous.

perpetuus, -a, -um, continuous, unbroken ; in perpetuum, for ever.

persaepe *adv.*, often.

persequor, -i, -secutus, pursue.

perspicio -ere, -spexi, -spectum, perceive, learn.

perterreo (2), frighten thoroughly.

perterritus, -a, -um, alarmed, daunted.

pertimesco, -ere, -mui, fear, dread.

pertineo, -ere, -ui, pertain to, concern.

perturbo (1), throw into confusion, confound.

pervenio, -ire, -veni, -ventum, arrive at, reach.

pestis, -is, *f.*, scourge, pest ; plague spot (I, 30).

petitio, -ionis, *f.*, attack.

peto, -ere, -ivi, -ii, -itum, attack.

petulantia, -ae, *f.*, impudence, wantonness.

pexus, -a, -um, combed.

Picenus, -a, -um, of Picenum (*northern Italy*).

pietas, -tatis, *f.*, devotion, duty, loyalty.

pl., *abbreviat. for* plebis *or* plebum.

placeo (2), *with dat.*, be pleasing to ; placet mihi, it seems right to me = it is my opinion ; (*of decrees, etc.*) it is resolved, determined.

placo (1), reconcile, appease.

plane, *adv.*, clearly, distinctly ; completely (II, 11).

plebs, plebis, *f.*, the people, the commons.

plurimus, -a, -um, *superl. of* multus, most.

poena, -ae, *f.*, penalty, punishment.

polliceor (2), promise.

pono, -ere, posui, positum, put, place ; pitch (*of camp*).

pontifex, -icis, high priest ; pontiff : p. maximus, chief pontiff.

popina, -ae, *f.*, tavern, den.

populus, -i, *m.*, people.

porta, -ae, *f.*, gate.

possessio, -ionis, *f.*, property, estate.

possum, posse, potui, be able, can.

post, *prep. with acc.*, after.

postea, *adv.*, afterwards, after.

posteritas, -tatis, *f.*, after ages, posterity ; in posteritatem, in the future.

postremus, -a, -um, last.

postulo (1), ask, demand.

potestas, -tatis, *f.*, power.

potior (4), *with gen.*, take possession of ; hold.

potius, *compar. adv.*, rather ; potius quam, rather than.

prae, *prep. with abl.*, in comparison with ; compared with.

praecipio, -ere, -cepi, -ceptum, enjoin, direct, bid, order.

praeclarus, -a, -um, very noble, glorious, famous.

praedator, -oris, *m.*, plunderer, pillager.

praedico (1), declare, proclaim.

praedico, -ere, -dixi, -dictum, foretell, predict.

praedium, -i, *n.*, estate.

praefero, -ferre, -tuli, -latum, carry in front.

praemitto, -ere, -misi, -missum, send on, ahead, *or* in front.

Praeneste, -is, *n.,* Praeneste (*town in Latium*).

praesens, -ntis, present.

praesentia, -ae, *f.,* presence.

praesertim, *adv.,* especially.

praesidium, -i, *n.,* defence ; garrison ; bodyguard (I, 11).

praestolor (1), wait for.

praeter, *prep. with acc.,* contrary to.

praeterea, *adv.,* further, besides, moreover.

praetereo, -ire, -ii, -itum, pass over, neglect.

praetermitto, -ere, -misi, -missum, pass over, make no mention of.

praetextus, -a, -um, bordered with purple ; *as noun,* **praetexta, -ae,** *f.,* the toga praetexta (*worn by the higher magistrates*).

praetor, -oris, *m.,* praetor.

praetorius, -a, -um, of a praetor *or* general ; **praetoria cohors,** bodyguard of a general.

precor (1), pray.

premo, -ere, pressi, pressum, press hard.

pridem, *adv.,* long since ; **iam pridem,** long ago.

pridie, *adv.,* on the day before.

primo, *adv.,* at first, firstly.

primum, *adv.,* first, in the first place.

primus, -a, -um, first.

princeps, -cipis, *m.,* chief person, leader: *pl.,* chief *or* leading men.

prior, prius, former, previous ; **priore nocte** (I, 8), the night before last.

pristinus, -a, -um, former.

privatus, -a, -um, private, personal ; *as noun,* a private person *or* citizen.

pro, *prep. with abl.,* on behalf of.

probo (1), prove, approve of.

procul, *adv.,* at a distance, from afar.

prodigium, -i, *n.,* portent ; unnatural person.

proelium, -i, *n.,* battle, engagement.

profectio, -ionis, *f.,* a setting out, departure.

profecto, *adv.,* assuredly, really.

profero, -ferre, -tuli, -latum, bring forward.

proficio, -ere, -feci, -fectum, effect, gain.

proficiscor, -i, -fectus, set out, depart, start.

profiteor, -eri, -fessus, profess, offer.

profligo (1), overcome, crush.

profugio, -ere, -fugi, flee from, flee away.

profundo, -ere, -fudi, -fusum, waste, dissipate, squander.

progredior, -i, -gressus, advance.

prohibeo (2), check, restrain, prevent.

proicio, -ere, -ieci, -iectum, throw *or* cast forth *or* away.

proinde, *adv.,* therefore, accordingly.

promitto, -ere, -misi, -missum, promise.

propago (1), extend, preserve.

prope, *adv.,* almost, nearly.

proprius, -a, -um, *with gen.,* one's own ; suited to, in keeping with.

propter, *prep. with acc.,* on account of.

proscriptio, -ionis, *f.,* notice of sale (II, 21) ; confiscation (II, 20).

prosequor, -i, -secutus, accompany, escort.

prospicio, -ere, -spexi, -spectum, look out for ; foresee.

prostratus, -a, -um, *perf. part. pass. of* prosterno, overthrown, destroyed.

provideo, -ere, -vidi, -visum, *with dat.*, see to, make provision *or* preparation for.

provincia, -ae, *f.*, province.

proximus, -a, -um, nearest, next ; previous, last ; **proxima nocte,** last night.

prudens, -ntis, wise, sensible.

prudentia, -ae, *f.*, knowledge, good sense, wisdom.

pruina, -ae, *f.*, frost.

publice, *adv.*, on behalf of the state ; on the part of the state (I, 11).

Publicius, -i, *m.*, associate of Catiline.

publicus, -a, -um, public ; res publica, rei publicae, *f.*, the state.

pudicitia, -ae, *f.*, modesty, virtue.

pudicus, -a, -um, modest, pure, virtuous.

pudor, -oris, *m.*, modesty, honour.

puer, -eri, *m.*, boy.

pugno (1), fight.

pulcher, -chra, -chrum, beautiful, fine, handsome.

purgo (1), cleanse, purify.

purpura, -ae, *f.*, the purple, the purple robe.

puto (1), think, suppose.

Q

Q., *abbreviat. for* Quintus, Roman praenomen.

quaero, -ere, -sivi, -situm, ask, seek.

quaeso, -ere, -ivi, -itum, beg, pray, beseech.

quaestio, -ionis, *f.*, inquiry ; *in pl.*, law-courts.

qualis, -e, *correlative pron.* or *adj.*, as.

quam, *adv.*, how ; **tam . . . quam,** so much . . . as ; *in comparisons*, than ; *with superlatives*, as . . . as possible ; **quam primum,** as soon as possible.

quam ob rem, wherefore.

quamquam, *conj.*, although, though ; and yet, moreover.

quantus, -a, -um, how great *or* big.

quare, *adv.*, wherefore.

quartus, -a, -um, fourth.

quattuor, four.

-que, *enclitic conj.*, and.

quem ad modum, *interrog. adv.*, how? *correlative adv.*, as.

querimonia, -ae, *f.*, complaint.

queror, -i, questus, complain.

qui, quae, quod, *relative pronoun*, who, which, that.

qui, quae, quod, *interrog. adj.*, which? what?

quia, *conj.*, because.

quid, *neut. of* quis, what? *as adv.*, why? how? nay more.

quidam, quaedam, quoddam, *indef. pronoun* ; a certain man, someone ; *as adj.*, a certain.

quidem, *adv.*, indeed ; **ne . . . quidem,** not even.

quiesco, -ere, -evi, -etum, keep silent *or* quiet.

quietus, -a, -um, at rest, quiet, undisturbed.

quin, *conj.*, nay more.

quintus, -a, -um, fifth.

Quirites, -um, *m. pl.,* Quirites, i.e. the Romans, Roman people.

quis, quid, *interrog. pron.,* who? which? what?

quis, qua, quid, *indefin. pron.,* anyone, anything, someone, something.

quisnam, *interrog. pron.,* who then? what, pray?

quisquam, quaequam, quidquam *or* **quicquam,** *indefin. pron., usually after neg.,* anyone, anything.

quisque, quaeque, quidque (*adj.* **quodque**), *indefin. pron.,* each, a man; **unus quisque,** each individual.

quisquis, -quid (*or* **quic**)**quid,** *relat. pron.,* whoever, whatever.

quo, *interrog. and relat. adv.,* whither, where, to which place; **quo usque,** how far?

quod, *conj.,* because, in that; **quodsi,** but if.

quondam, *adv.,* once, formerly.

quoniam, *conj.,* since, seeing that.

quoque, *adv.,* also, too.

quot, *indecl. adj.,* how many.

quotiens, *adv.,* how often, how many times.

quotienscumque, *adv.,* as often as.

R

rapina, -ae, *f.,* robbery, plunder.

rapio, -ere, rapui, raptum, seize, snatch; hurry *or* hasten off.

ratio, -ionis, *f.,* way; reflection (I, 22).

recens, -ntis, fresh.

recipio, -ere, -cepi, -ceptum, receive.

recognosco, -ere, -gnovi, -gnitum, review.

recondo, -ere, -didi, -ditum, bury in.

recreo (1), refresh, revive.

recta, *adv.,* straightway.

redeo, -ire, -ii, -itum, return, come back.

redimio (4), bind round, wreathe.

redundo (1), redound to, fall upon.

refero, -ferre, rettuli, relatum, show (*of gratitude*), I, 28; put (*a question to the senate*) (I, 20, II, 26).

regie, *adv.,* tyrannically.

relevo (1), (lift up), relieve.

relinquo, -ere, -liqui, -lictum, leave, leave behind.

reliquus, -a, -um, remaining; *in pl.,* the rest.

remaneo, -ere, -mansi, -mansum, remain behind.

remoror (1), keep waiting (I, 4).

repello, -ere, reppuli, repulsum, drive back; repulse, baffle (I, 27).

repentinus, -a, -um, sudden.

reperio, -ire, repperi, repertum, find out, discover.

reprimo, -ere, -pressi, -pressum, check, crush.

repudio (1), reject.

res, rei, *f.,* thing; **res publica, rei publicae,** *f.,* the state; **summa res publica,** the supreme welfare of the state; **quam ob rem,** wherefore.

reseco, -are, -cui, -ctum, cut off; check, restrain.

resideo, -ere, -sedi, remain behind.

respondeo, -ere, -di, -sum, answer, reply.

reticeo (2), keep *or* be silent.

retorqueo, -ere, -si, -tum, twist *or* turn back.

revoco (1), call back.

rex, regis, *m.,* king.
robur, -oris, *n.,* might, power.
robustus, -a -um, strong, hardy.
rogo (1), ask, ask for (I, 9) ; pass (*a law*) (I, 28).
Roma, -ae, *f.,* Rome.
Romanus, -a, -um, Roman ; *as noun,* a Rcman.
Romulus, -i, *m.,* Romulus (*legendary founder of Rome*).
ruina, -ae, *f.,* downfall, collapse, ruin.
rusticus, -a, -um, rough, rude, boorish.

S

sacer, -cra, -crum, sacred.
sacra, -orum, *n. pl.,* sacred rites.
sacrarium, -i, *n.,* shrine, chapel.
sacrosanctus, -a, -um, most holy *or* sacred.
saeculum, -i, *n.,* age, generation.
saepe, *adv.,* often ; *compar.* saepius, repeatedly ; *superl.,* saepissime.
sagax, -acis, shrewd.
salto (1), dance.
salus, -utis, *f.,* welfare, preservation.
saluto (1), greet, salute.
salvus, -a, -um, safe, unharmed.
sanctus, -a, -um, sacred, awful, venerable, revered.
sane, *adv.,* truly, certainly.
sanguis, -inis, *m.,* blood.
sano (1), cure, heal, make whole.
sanus, -a, -um, sound, whole, healthy.
satelles, -itis, *c.,* attendant, servant.
satis, *as indecl. noun and adj.,* enough ; *as adv.,* enough, sufficiently.

satisfacio, -ere, -feci, -factum, give satisfaction (*often with dat.*).
Saturninus, -i, *m.,* L. Appuleius Saturninus.
saucius, -a, -um, wounded.
scaena, -ae, *f.,* the stage.
scelerate, *adv.,* wickedly, villainously.
sceleratus, -a, -um, wicked ; *as noun,* a scoundrel.
scelus, -eris, *n.,* crime, sin.
scientia, -ae, *f.,* knowledge.
scilicet, *adv.,* of course (*often ironical*).
scio (4), know.
Scipio, -ionis, *m.,* P. Scipio Nasica.
scortum, -i, *n.,* harlot, prostitute.
se *or* **sese,** *reflex. pron.,* himself, herself, themselves.
secedo, -ere, -cessi, -cessum, withdraw, retire.
secerno, -ere, -crevi, -cretum, separate.
secum = cum se.
securis, -is, *f.,* axe.
sed, *conj.,* but.
seditio, -ionis, *f.,* sedition.
sedo (1), calm, quiet, appease.
seiungo, -ere, -nxi, -nctum, separate.
semen, -inis, *n.,* seed, germ.
seminarium, -i, *n.,* nursery, school.
semper, *adv.,* always, ever.
senator, -oris, *m.,* senator.
senatus, -us, *m.,* senate.
senex, senis, *m.,* old man.
sensus, -us, *m.,* feeling.
sententia, -ae, *f.,* opinion ; vote (*in the senate*).
sentina, -ae, *f.,* scum, refuse, (*lit.,* bilge-water).

sentio, -ire, sensi, sensum, feel, perceive, realise, think.

sequor, -i, secutus, follow.

sermo, -onis, *m.*, conversation, talk.

sero, *adv.*, late, too late ; *compar.*, serius.

sertum, -i, *n.*, garland, chaplet.

Servilius, -i, *m.*, C. Servilius Ahala (I, 3), *slayer of Sp. Maelius*, 440 B.C.

Servilius, -i, *m.*, C. Servilius Glaucia (I, 4) (*democrat and supporter of Saturninus*, 100 B.C.).

servio, (4), serve ; *with dat.*, serve the interests of, work for.

servo (1), save ; preserve (I, 25).

servus, -i, *m.*, servant, slave.

sese, *see* se.

Sestius, -i, *m.*, Publius Sestius.

severitas, -tatis, *f.*, severity.

si, *conj.*, if ; si minus, if not.

sic, *adv.*, so, thus.

sica, -ae, *f.*, dagger.

sicarius, -i, *m.*, assassin, murderer.

sicut, *adv.*, just as, as.

significatio, -ionis, *f.*, sign.

signum, -i, *n.*, standard.

silentium, -i, *n.*, silence.

sileo (2), be silent ; pass over in silence (I, 14).

silvestris, -e, wooded.

similis, -e, like, similar (*with gen. or dat.*).

simul, *adv.*, at once ; together ; simul atque, as soon as.

sin, *conj.*, if however, but if.

sine, *prep. with abl.*, without.

singuli, -ae, -a, one apiece, single.

sino, -ere, sivi, situm, suffer, allow.

sinus, -us, *m.*, bosom, intimacy.

sitis, -is, *f.*, thirst.

sobrius, -a, -um, sober.

societas, -tatis, *f.*, alliance ; conspiracy.

socius, -i, *m.*, comrade, ally.

sodalis, -is, *c.*, comrade, booncompanion.

soleo, -ere, solitus sum, *semi-dep.*, be accustomed, be wont.

solitudo, -inis, *f.*, loneliness, solitude.

solum, *adv.*, alone, only.

solus, -a, -um, alone.

solutior, *compar.* of solutus, -a, -um, lax, remiss.

somnus, -i, *m.*, sleep.

Sp., *abbrev. for* Spurius, Roman praenomen.

spargo, -ere, -si, -sum, sprinkle, spread.

species, -ei, *f.*, type, kind.

speculor (1), spy out, observe.

spero (1), hope, hope for.

spes, spei, *f.*, hope.

spiritus, -us, *m.*, air.

spolio (1), despoil.

sponte, *f.*, of free will.

Stator, -oris, *m.*, the Supporter, the Stayer, (*epithet of Jupiter*).

statuo, -ere, -ui, -utum, settle, determine.

status, -us, *m.*, state, position.

stirps, stirpis, *f.*, root.

sto, stare, steti, statum, stand ; stand firm, continue, (II, 21).

studeo (2), strive after, desire (*with dat.*).

studium, -i, *n.*, eagerness, zeal ; *in pl.*, pursuits, strong feelings.

stultus, -a, -um, foolish, stupid.

stuprum, -i, *n.*, debauchery.

suadeo, -ere, -si, -sum, advise, urge (*usually with dat.*).

subeo, -ire, -ivi *or* -ii, -itum, undergo.
subiector, -oris, *m.*, forger.
subito, *adv.*, suddenly.
subsellium, -i, *n.*, seat, bench.
subsidium, -i, *n.*, *in pl.*, means, resources.
succedo, -ere, -cessi, -cessum, take the place of, succeed.
suffero, -ferre, sustuli, sublatum, suffer.
Sulla, -ae, *m.*, L. Cornelius Sulla, (*Roman general, supporter of the senate, and dictator*, 80 B.C.).
sum, esse, fui, I am, exist.
summus, -a, -um, highest, greatest, most important, most distinguished ; supreme.
sumptuose, *adv.*, *compar.* sumptuosius, extravagantly.
sumptus, -us, *m.*, expense.
superior, -ioris, former, previous.
supero (1), overcome.
suppedito (1), supply, furnish.
supplicium, -i, *n.*, punishment, torture.
suscipio, -ere, -cepi, -ceptum, undertake.
suspectus, -a, -um, mistrusted, suspected.
suspicio, -ionis, *f.*, mistrust, suspicion.
suspicor (1), mistrust, suspect.
sustineo, -ere, -tinui, -tentum, support, bear up against.
suus, -a, -um, his, her, their own ; sui, -orum, *m. pl.*, his followers *or* supporters.

T

tabesco, -ere, -ui, pine away, languish.
tabula, -ae, *f.*, *in pl.*, public records (I, 4) ; tabulae novae, new account books, i.e. cancellation of debts.
taceo (2), be silent, keep silence.
taciturnitas, -tatis, *f.*, silence.
tacitus, -a, -um, silent.
taeter, -tra, -trum, noisome, dreadful.
talaris, -e, reaching to the ankles, long.
talis, -e, of such a kind, such : talis . . . qualis, of such a kind (*or* such) . . . as.
tam, *adv.*, so.
tamen, *conj.*, nevertheless, yet.
tametsi, *conj.*, although.
tamquam, *adv.*, as though, as if.
tandem, *adv.*, at length, at last : pray (I, 1).
tantus, -a, -um, so great ; so grave (I, 7).
tectum, -i, *n.*, house, dwelling.
tecum = cum te.
telum, -i, *n.*, weapon.
temeritas, -tatis, *f.*, rashness, recklessness.
temperantia, -ae, *f.*, sobriety, self-restraint, moderation.
tempestas, -tatis, *f.*, storm.
templum, -i, *n.*, temple, shrine.
tempto (1), attack, assail.
tempus, -oris, *n.*, time, season.
tenebrae, -arum, *f. pl.*, darkness, gloom.
teneo, -ere, -ui, tentum, hold, keep, hold fast ; beset (I, 6).
tenuis, -e, slender.
terra, -ae, *f.*, earth, land ; terra marique, on land and sea.
tertius, -a, -um, third.
testamentum, -i, *n.*, will.
Ti., *abbreviat. for* Tiberius, Roman praenomen.

timeo (2), fear.

timidus, -a, -um, nervous, fearful.

timor, -oris, *m.*, fear.

toga, -ae, *f.*, toga (*national dress of the Romans*).

togatus, -a, -um, wearing the toga, i.e. in civil life, as a citizen.

tolero (1), bear, endure.

tollo, -ere, sustuli, sublatum, take away, remove.

Tongilius, -i, *m.*, Tongilius, (*associate of Catiline*).

tot, *indecl.*, so many.

totiens, *adv.*, so many times.

totus, -a, -um, all, the whole : *often best translated as an adv.*, wholly, entirely.

transfero, -ferre, -tuli, -latum, carry across : turn (*one's right hand*) to (I, 24).

tribunal -alis, *n.*, tribunal.

tribunus, -i, *m.*, tribune (*of the people*), tribune.

triduum, -i, *n.*, three days, a period of three days.

triumpho (1), triumph.

trucido (1), slaughter, slay.

tu, you.

tuba, -ae, *f.*, war-trumpet.

Tullius, -i, *m.*, Tullius, name of a Roman gens, *or* clan.

Tullus, -i, *m.*, Lucius Volcatius Tullus (*consul with M'. Aemilius Lepidus in* 66 B.C).

tum, *adv.*, then.

tumultus, -us, *m.*, uproar, din ; alarm (*of war*) (I, 11).

tumulus, -i, *m.*, mound, hill.

tune = tu *with interrogative* -ne *attached.*

tunica, -ae, *f.*, tunic.

turbulentus, -a, -um, troublesome, seditious.

turpiter, *adv.*, *superl.* turpissime, disgracefully, shamefully, basely.

turpitudo, -inis, *f.*, dishonour, infamy.

tuto, *adv.*, in safety, safely.

tutus, -a, -um, safe.

tuus, -a, -um, your ; tui, -orum, *m. pl.*, your friends *or* followers.

tyrannus, -i, *m.*, despot, tyrant.

U

ubi (*interrogative*), *adv.*, where ? strengthened by nam, ubinam.

ulciscor, -i, ultus, punish.

ullus, -a, -um, any, any one.

umquam, *adv.*, ever, at any time.

una, *adv.*, at the same time, in company with.

undique, *adv.*, from *or* on all sides, from every side.

unguentum, -i, *n.*, perfume.

universus, -a, -um, whole, universal.

unus, -a, -um, one, single ; alone ; unus quisque, each individual.

urbanus, -a, -um, of a city *or* town ; praetor urbanus, the city praetor.

urbs, urbis, *f.*, city ; *especially* Rome.

usque, *adv.*, right on ; usque ad, as far as, even to (I, 21) ; quo usque, how far ? (I, 1).

usura, -ae, *f.*, enjoyment (*of a thing*) (I, 29) ; interest.

ut, *as conj.*, *with indicat.*, as, when ; *with subjunct.*, in order that, so that, that ; *as adv.*, *in comparisons*, as, just as.

uterque, -traque, -trumque, each (*of two*), both.

utilis, -e, useful, expedient.

utinam, *adv.*, Oh that! would that! (*introducing wishes*).

utor, -i, usus, *with abl.*, use, enjoy.

uxor, -oris, *f.*, wife.

V

vacillo (1), hesitate, waver, totter.

vacuefacio, -ere, -feci, -factum, leave empty.

vadimonium, -i, *n.*, recognisance, bail.

vagina, -ae, *f.*, scabbard, sheath.

valde, *adv.*, strongly, earnestly.

valeo (2), be strong; have sufficient strength *or* power to.

Valerius, -i, *m.*, Lucius Valerius.

varius, -a, -um, varied, various, diverse, mixed.

vastatio, -ionis, *f.*, devastation, laying waste.

vastitas, -tatis, *f.*, devastation, desolation.

vasto (1), devastate, ruin.

vectigal, -alis, *n.*, tax.

vehemens, -ntis, vigorous, strong.

vehementer, *adv.*, strongly, severely.

vel . . . vel, either . . . or. vel, or.

velum, -i, *n.*, veil, covering.

vena, -ae, *f.*, vein.

veneficus, -i, *m.*, poisoner.

venenum, -i, *n.*, poison.

veneror (1), reverence; entreat (II, 29).

venio, -ire, veni, ventum, come.

verbum, -i, *n.*, word.

vere, *adv.*, truly, really.

vereor (2), fear.

vero, *adv.*, in truth, indeed.

versor (1), dwell, remain; be engaged in.

verum, *adv.*, but in truth, but.

verus, -a, -um, true, real.

vesperam, ad, towards evening.

vester, -tra, -trum, your.

vetus, veteris, old, long-standing.

vexatio, -ionis, *f.*, harassing.

vexo (1), harass, annoy.

via, -ae, *f.*, road.

vibro (1), poise, (*of daggers*) shake.

vicesimus, -a, -um, twentieth.

vicinus, -i, *m.*, neighbour.

videlicet, *adv.*, forsooth, of course (*usually ironical*).

video, -ere, vidi, visum, see, perceive; *in pass.*, seem.

vigilia, -ae, *f.*, watching; *in pl.*, guards, patrols, sentinels.

vigilo (1), be watchful *or* vigilant.

vilis, -e, cheap, worthless.

vinclum, -i, (*also* vinculum), *n.*, chain; *in plur.*, prison.

vinco, -ere, vici, victum, conquer, defeat.

vindex, -icis, avenging.

vindico (1), avenge, punish.

vinum, -i, *n.*, wine.

vir, viri, *m.*, man.

virtus, -utis, *f.*, courage; worth, excellence; virtue.

vis, vim, vi; *pl.*, vires, -ium, -ibus, *in sing.*, force, violence; *in pl.*, power, might, strength.

viscus, -eris, *n.*, vitals.

vita, -ae, *f.*, life.

vitium, -i, *n.*, vice, crime.

vito (1), avoid, shun.

vivo, -ere, -xi, -ctum, live.

vivus, -a, -um, alive, living.

vix, *adv.*, with difficulty, scarcely; vixdum, hardly, scarcely yet.

voco (1), call, summon.
volito (1), fly around, flit, hover.
volo, velle, volui, will, wish.
voluntas, -tatis, *f.*, will, wish.
voluptas, -tatis, *f.*, pleasure, joy.

votum, -i, *n.*, prayer; curse (II, 18).
vox, vocis, *f.*, voice; *in pl.*, words.
vulnero (1), wound.
vultus, -us, *m.*, countenance, look.